Using the Standards
Algebra

Grade 5

by
Melissa Warner Hale

Published by Instructional Fair
an imprint of
Frank Schaffer Publications®

Instructional Fair

Author: Melissa Warner Hale
Editor: Karen Thompson

Frank Schaffer Publications®

Instructional Fair is an imprint of Frank Schaffer Publications.

Send all inquiries to:
Frank Schaffer Publications
820 Orion Place
Columbus, OH 43240-2111

Using the Standards: Algebra—grade 5

ISBN: 0-7424-2885-0

6 7 8 9 10 MAZ 09 08 07

Table of Contents

Introduction

NCTM Standards: This book focuses on the National Council of Teachers of Mathematics (NCTM) content standards of Algebra. The activities are divided into four main sections, based on the NCTM Algebra standards. NCTM defines the standards as follows.

Patterns and Functions: Students will learn to understand patterns, relations and functions. For grades 3–5, this includes describing, extending, and making generalizations about geometric and numeric patterns as well as representing and analyzing patterns and functions using words, tables, and graphs.

Situations and Structures: Students will be able to represent and analyze mathematical situations and structures using algebraic symbols. The specific skills used in grades 3–5 are identifying mathematical properties and using them to compute with whole numbers, representing an unknown quantity with a letter or symbol, and expressing mathematical relationships using equations.

Models: Students will use mathematical models to represent and understand numerical relationships. In grades 3–5 this includes using objects and representations such as graphs, tables, and equations.

Changes in Context: Students will learn to analyze change in various contexts. For grades 3–5, this includes investigating how change in one variable relates to a change in a second variable. Students will also identify, describe, and compare situations with constant or varying rates of change.

Each activity in the book also incorporates at least one of the five NCTM process standards:

 Problem Solving

 Communication

 Reasoning and Proof

 Connections

Representation

Each activity is referenced in the **NCTM Algebra Standards Correlation Chart** on page 6, which identifies the specific content skills and process standards found in that activity.

Pretest: This short pretest contains a representative sampling of activities similar to those used throughout this book. Give this pretest at one time, or present one problem at a time over a series of days. Students may work on these problems individually, in pairs, or in groups. The purpose of the pretest is to provide insights into the content knowledge and problem-solving strategies students already possess. The emphasis should not be on the number of "right" answers. Instead, encourage students to try their best and write down their ideas. These problems can also provide opportunities for class discussion as students share their thought processes with one another.

Introduction (cont.)

Workbook Pages: Activities can be done independently, in pairs, or in groups. Problems may be broken into parts, with class discussion following student work. Encourage students to create their own strategies for solving the problems. Many activities will lead into subjects that could be investigated or discussed further as a class. You may want to compare different solution methods or discuss how to select a valid solution method for a particular problem. Each activity ends with a **Think** or **Do More** prompt. They are designed as prompts for discussion or journal entries, as jumping off points for further exploration, or as connections to other areas of mathematics.

Create Your Own Problems: At the end of each of the four sections, students will be prompted to create mathematical problems utilizing the concepts learned in that section. You may wish to have students try to solve one another's problems, or even choose some of the student-created problems to be used on a test or for homework.

Check Your Skills: These activities provide a representative sample of the skills developed throughout each section. This can be used as additional practice or as a posttest for the section.

Cumulative Posttest: This is a short posttest providing a representative sample of problems used throughout the book. It may be used for assessment or extra practice. The test can be given all at one time or may be split up over several days.

Vocabulary Cards: Use the vocabulary cards to familiarize students with mathematical language. The pages may be copied, cut, and pasted onto index cards. Paste the front and back on the same index card to make flash cards, or paste each side on separate cards to use in matching games and activities.

Assessment: Assessment is an integral part of the learning process and can include observations, conversations, interviews, interactive journals, writing prompts, and independent quizzes or tests. Classroom discussions help students learn the difference between mediocre, good, and excellent responses. Scoring guides can help analyze students' responses. The following is one possible scoring rubric. Modify this rubric as necessary to fit specific problems.

1—Student understands the problem and knows what he/she is being asked to find.
2—Student selects an appropriate strategy or process to solve the problem.
3—Student is able to model the problem with appropriate graphs, tables, pictures, computations, or equations.
4—Student is able to clearly explain or demonstrate his/her thinking and reasoning.

NCTM Algebra Standards Correlation Chart

	Problem Solving	Reasoning and Proof	Communication	Connections	Representation
Patterns and Functions describe and extend patterns	10, 14–15	13, 16–19	10, 12, 14–15	9, 11	9–13, 16–19
represent patterns and functions	24–27, 30	20–23, 27	20–26, 28	28–29, 31	20–23, 29–31
Situations and Structures identify and use properties	38–39, 45	34–37, 41–43	34–35, 38–39, 44	40, 42–47	42–44
variables	48–49, 56–59	56, 58–59	49, 53–54, 57	52, 55, 58–59	48–57
equations	62–65, 68–72	62–63, 66–67	66–67, 70–71	60–61, 64–72	60–61, 64–65, 68–72
Models model with objects & use representations	45, 76–79	18–19, 78–83	78–83	45, 76–83	18–19, 76–79
Changes in Context changes in related variables	90–91	92–93	90–95	87–95	87–89, 91–95
constant and varying rates of change	96–97, 102–105	100–101	96–99, 100–103	96–99, 100–105	96–99, 100–101, 104–105

*The pretest, posttest, Create Your Own Problems, and Check Your Skills pages are not included on this chart, but contain a representative sampling of the process standards.

Name ______________________ Date ____________

Pretest

1. Fill in the next three numbers in the pattern. Identify the type of pattern (repeating, growing, or decreasing). Then give a rule for the pattern.

a. 1,268 1,079 890 701 ______ ______ ______

Rule: ____

b. 6 24 96 384 ______ ______ ______

Rule: ____

c. 25 81 81 25 81 81 ______ ______ ______

Rule: ____

2. A function machine uses a rule to change numbers. Look for a pattern between the IN and OUT numbers in the table. Fill in the missing numbers. Write the rule.

IN	84		54	36	72	30
OUT		15	9	6		5

Rule: ____

3. Name the property—commutative, associative, or distributive—that was used to rewrite each equation.

a. 625 + (74 + 38) = (625 + 74) + 38 ______________________

b. 625 + 74 + 38 = 74 + 625 + 38 ______________________

c. (625 + 74) x 38 = 625 x 38 + 74 x 38 ______________________

4. Each letter stands for a different number. Find the number that makes each equation true.

a. 3 x *V* + 328 = 970 __________ **b.** *T* ÷ 18 = 87 __________

c. 25 x *W* + 66 = 2,366 __________ **d.** 942 – *S* = 700 __________

5. There are 60 pieces of candy in a bag. There are twice as many chocolates as there are licorice. Chocolates make up half the bag of candy. There are 3 fewer peppermints than there are sour balls. How many pieces of each type are in the bag?

S = # of sour balls *C* = # of chocolates *L* = # of licorice *P* = # of Peppermints

S = __________ *C* = __________ *L* = __________ *P* = __________

Name ______________________ Date ____________

Pretest (cont.)

6. A car travels 600 miles at an average speed of *R* miles per hour.

a. If *T* is the time it takes for the car to drive 600 miles, write an equation showing the relationship between *T* and *R*.

b. Complete the table below showing the average speed, *R*, the car would have to travel to make the trip in the time given.

T (hrs.)	7	8	9	10	11	12	13	14	15
R (mi/hr.)									

c. What happens to the speed as the time increases? ______________________

d. Does the speed change at a constant rate, a decreasing rate, or an increasing rate? How do you know? ______________________

7. A rectangular garden has sides that are 12 ft. and 14 ft. long.

a. What is the perimeter and area of the garden? $P =$ __________ $A =$ __________

b. If each side of the garden is doubled, what will happen to the perimeter? Write an equation showing this relationship. Let *P* represent the original perimeter and let *N* represent the new perimeter. ______________________

c. If each side of the garden is doubled, what will happen to the area? Write an equation showing this relationship. Let *A* be the original area of the garden and let *M* be the new area of the garden. ______________________

8. A store is having a clearance sale. Each item in the store is on sale for 30% off.

a. Let *R* represent the original retail price of an item and let *D* represent the discount. Write an equation showing the relationship between the original price and the amount of the discount. ______________________

b. Which graph best shows the relationship between the retail price and the amount of the discount? Explain why you chose that graph. ______________________

A.

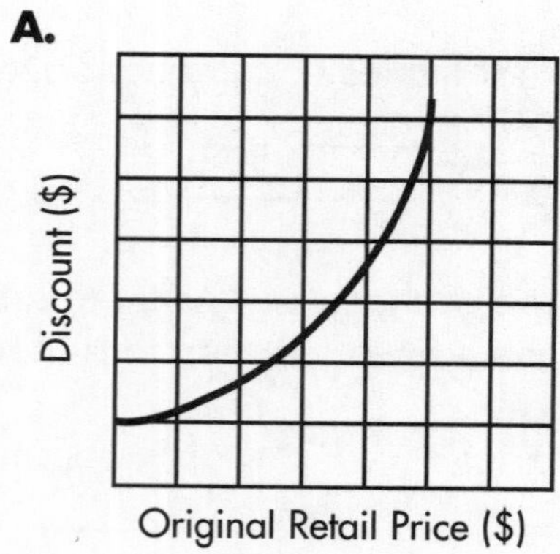

B.

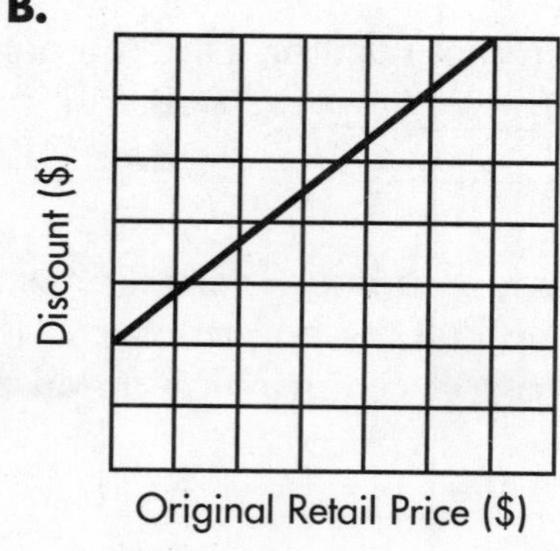

C.

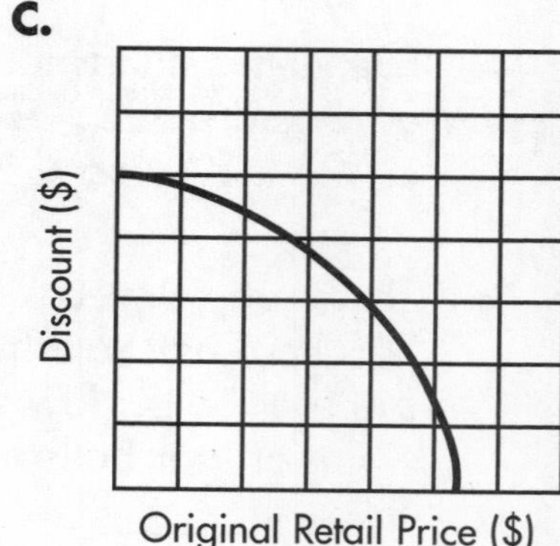

0-7424-2885-0 *Using the Standards—Algebra*

Name ______________________ Date ____________

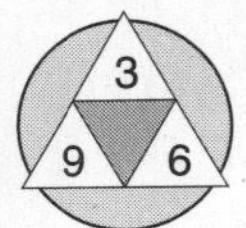

Move to the Rhythm

Dances often contain steps or movements that repeat in a certain pattern. Follow the directions below to create dance rhythms.

1. Choose 4 different dance movements. These could be clapping, stepping forward, stepping back, bending, turning right or left, hopping, or anything else. Choose a letter—A, B, C, or D—to represent each movement. Follow one of the rhythm patterns below. Practice your dance rhythm by repeating the movements over and over. Then try the other rhythm patterns.

   a. A A B B

   b. A B B C

   c. A B B C C D

   d. A A B C D D

   e. A B C D

   f. A B B B C C D

2. Assign a different movement to each letter. Use the rhythm patterns from problem 1 to create a new dance with these movements. How are the dances similar? How are they different?

DO MORE

Create your own dance rhythms that have a pattern that is different than those listed in problem 1. Choose a different letter for each movement. Write the letter pattern that matches your dance movements.

Name ______________________ Date __________

Jumpin' Jigsaws

The table below has horizontal, vertical, and diagonal patterns. The missing squares are scattered around the page. Cut out the squares and paste them in the table to complete the patterns.

DO MORE

Describe all the patterns you see in the table.

0-7424-2885-0 *Using the Standards—Algebra*

Name ____________________ Date __________

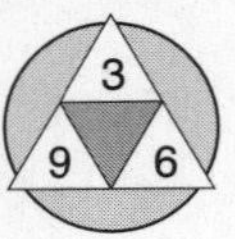

Shape Up

Find the repeating pattern. Draw in the missing shapes. Describe the patterns using the letters A and B.

1. ______ ______ ______ ______

pattern: ____________________

2. ______ ______ ______ ______

pattern: ____________________

3. ______ ______ ______ ______

pattern: ____________________

4. ______ ______ ______ ______

pattern: ____________________

DO MORE

Name each of the different shapes used in the patterns above. What do all of these shapes have in common? What do you notice about the shapes used in each problem?

0-7424-2885-0 *Using the Standards—Algebra*

Name ______________________ Date ___________

Nutty Numerals

Find the **repeating number pattern**. Insert the missing numbers. Then use letters to show the same pattern. Replace each number with the letter A, B, or C.

1. _____ 23 14 23 23 _____ _____ 23 _____

Letter pattern: ______________________________

2. 45 _____ 11 45 37 _____ _____ 37 _____

Letter pattern: ______________________________

3. 66 _____ _____ 84 66 _____ 84 _____ 66 66

Letter pattern: ______________________________

4. 92 54 _____ 87 92 54 54 _____ _____ _____

Letter pattern: ______________________________

5. _____ 28 48 28 _____ 48 _____ _____ _____

Letter pattern: ______________________________

6. 105 _____ 354 _____ 99 354 105 _____ _____

Letter pattern: ______________________________

THINK

Compare the above patterns. Describe any similarities and differences.

0-7424-2885-0 *Using the Standards—Algebra*

Name ______________________ Date ____________

It's a Match

Match each shape pattern to its corresponding number and symbol pattern.

______ ______ 1.

______ ______ 2.

______ ______ 3.

______ ______ 4.

______ ______ 5.

A.

B.

C.

D.

E.

I. 15 23 9 15 23 9

II. 74 74 55 74 74 55

III. 38 38 19 19 38 38

IV. 67 11 11 67 11 11

V. 93 46 93 46 93 46

THINK

How did you choose matching patterns? Give evidence that shows your answers are right.

Name ______________________ Date ____________

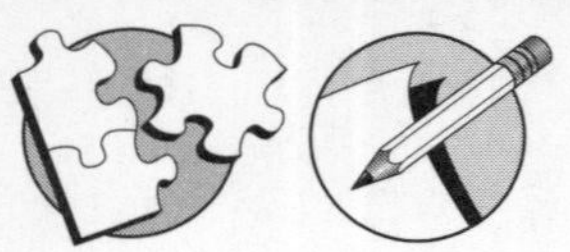

Growing and Shrinking

In a **growing pattern**, the numbers get larger in a predictable way.

In a **decreasing pattern**, the numbers get smaller in a predictable way.

Find the pattern. Use the pattern to find the next three numbers in the sequence. Write **growing** or **decreasing** next to each pattern. Then use words to describe how to find the next number in the pattern.

1. 302 374 446 518 ______ ______ ______ ____________

   Pattern description: ______________________________

2. 7,950 7,322 6,694 ______ ______ ______ ____________

   Pattern description: ______________________________

3. 3,129 2,689 2,249 1,809 ______ ______ ______ ____________

   Pattern description: ______________________________

4. 769 824 879 934 989 ______ ______ ______ ____________

   Pattern description: ______________________________

DO MORE

Create your own pattern. See if a friend can find your pattern.

Name ______________________ Date __________

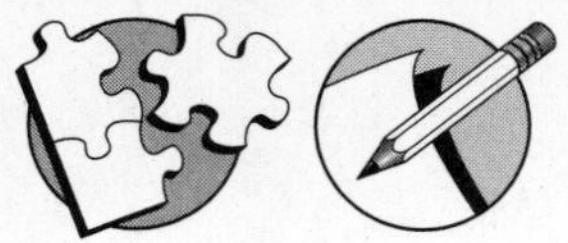

Climbing and Falling

In a **growing pattern**, the numbers get larger in a predictable way.

In a **decreasing pattern**, the numbers get smaller in a predictable way.

Find the pattern. Use the pattern to find the next three numbers in the sequence. Write **growing** or **decreasing** next to each pattern. Then use words to describe how to find the next number in the pattern.

1. 18 90 450 2,250 _______ _______ _______ ______________

Pattern description: ______________________________

2. 281,250 56,250 11,250 2,250 _______ _______ _______ _______

Pattern description: ______________________________

3. 1,835,008 229,376 28,672 3,584 _______ _______ _______ _______

Pattern description: ______________________________

4. 7 56 448 3,584 _______ _______ _______ ______________

Pattern description: ______________________________

THINK

How are patterns 1 and 2 related? How are patterns 3 and 4 related?

Name ______________________ Date ____________

By the Rules

A **rule** describes the process used to create the pattern.

Example: 10 28 46 64 82 Rule: + 18

Find the patterns. Fill in the missing numbers in the pattern. Write the rule for each pattern.

1. 3 ______ ______ 192 768 3,072 ______ ______

Rule: ______________________

2. ______ 35,000,000 3,500,000 ______ 35,000 3,500 ______ ______

Rule: ______________________

3. ______ 7,942 7,609 7,276 ______ ______ ______ 5,944

Rule: ______________________

4. 340 ______ ______ 898 1,084 1,270 ______ ______

Rule: ______________________

DO MORE

Prove that the numbers you chose and your rule work in the pattern. Start with the first number in the pattern. Use your rule to find the next number. Continue until you have found 8 numbers. Do these numbers match the ones given?

Name ______________________ Date ___________

A Rule in Time

A **rule** describes the process used to create the pattern.

Example: 73 61 49 37 25 Rule: – 12

Find the patterns. Fill in the missing numbers in the pattern. Write the rule for each pattern.

1. 55 94 133 172 _______ _______ _______ _______

   Rule: ______________________

2. _______ 5,103 1,701 _______ _______ 63 21 _______

   Rule: ______________________

3. 905 831 _______ 683 609 _______ _______ _______

   Rule: ______________________

4. _______ _______ 80 320 1,280 _______ _______ 81,920

   Rule: ______________________

DO MORE

Prove that the numbers you chose and your rule work in the pattern. Start with the first number in the pattern. Use your rule to find the next number. Continue until you have found 8 numbers. Do these numbers match the ones given?

0-7424-2885-0 *Using the Standards—Algebra*

Name ______________________ Date __________

Building Blocks

Materials: cubes

Build each of the following models.

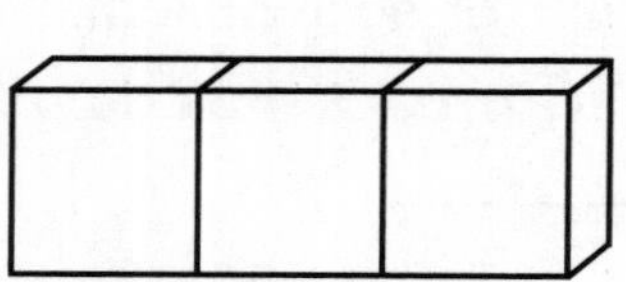

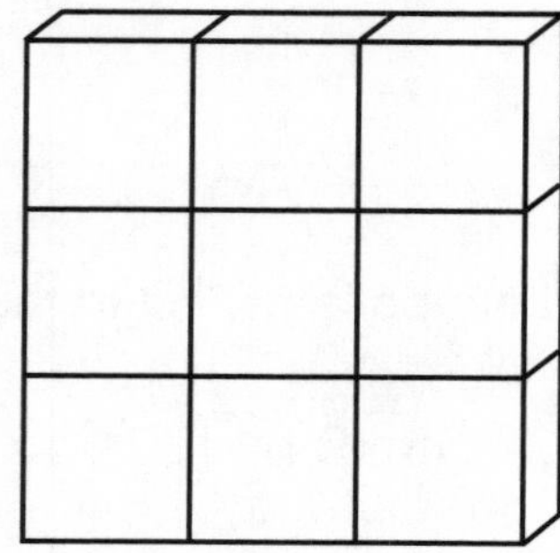

1. Find the volume of each model. Write the volume of each model in order on the line below.

   Volume: ____

2. Find the pattern. Write the rule.

   Rule: ____

3. Use the rule to find the volume of the next 3 models in the pattern.

   ____

Name ______________________ Date __________

Building Blocks (cont.)

4. How can you prove that your answers to problem 3 are correct?

5. Find the surface area of each model. Write the surface area of each model in order on the line below.

   Surface Area: ____

6. Find the pattern. Write the rule.

   Rule: ____

7. Use the rule to find the surface area of the next 3 models in the pattern.

   ____

8. How can you prove that your answers to problem 7 are correct?

THINK

How are the patterns for volume and surface area similar? How are they different?

Name ______________________ Date ____________

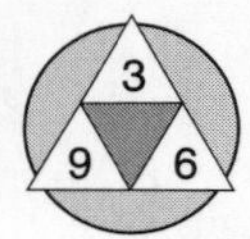

Changing Constantly

If a pattern has a **constant rate of change**, then the difference between each pair of numbers in the pattern is the same.

Find the rule for each growing pattern. Then answer the questions.

1. 6 37 68 99 130

Rule: ______________________

a. Find the difference between each pair of numbers in the pattern.

130 – 99 = ____________ 99 – 68 = ____________

68 – 37 = ____________ 37 – 6 = ____________

b. Does this pattern have a constant rate of change? Explain.

2. 6 18 54 162 486

Rule: ______________________

a. Find the difference between each pair of numbers in the pattern.

486 – 162 = ____________ 162 – 54 = ____________

54 – 18 = ____________ 18 – 6 = ____________

b. Does this pattern have a constant rate of change? Explain.

0-7424-2885-0 *Using the Standards—Algebra*

Name ______________________ Date ____________

Changing Constantly (cont.)

3. 4 24 144 864 5,184

Rule: ____________________________

a. Find the difference between each pair of numbers in the pattern.

5,184 − 864 = ______________ 864 − 144 = ______________

144 − 24 = ______________ 24 − 4 = ______________

b. Does this pattern have a constant rate of change? Explain.

4. 112 134 156 178 200

Rule: ____________________________

a. Find the difference between each pair of numbers in the pattern.

200 − 178 = ______________ 178 − 156 = ______________

156 − 134 = ______________ 134 − 112 = ______________

b. Does this pattern have a constant rate of change? Explain.

THINK

What can you say about patterns where the rule is to add the same number every time? What can you say about patterns where the rule is to multiply the same number every time?

Name ______________________ Date ____________

Steady Does It

If a pattern has a **constant rate of change**, then the difference between each pair of numbers in the pattern is the same.

Find the rule for each decreasing pattern. Then answer the questions.

1. 712 656 600 544 488

Rule: ______________________

a. Find the difference between each pair of numbers in the pattern.

712 – 656 = ____________ 656 – 600 = ____________

600 – 544 = ____________ 544 – 488 = ____________

b. Does this pattern have a constant rate of change? Explain.

2. 768 192 48 12 3

Rule: ______________________

a. Find the difference between each pair of numbers in the pattern.

768 – 192 = ____________ 192 – 48 = ____________

48 – 12 = ____________ 12 – 3 = ____________

b. Does this pattern have a constant rate of change? Explain.

Name ______________________ Date ____________

Steady Does It (cont.)

3. 548 479 410 341 272

Rule: ______________________

a. Find the difference between each pair of numbers in the pattern.

548 – 479 = ____________ 479 – 410 = ____________

410 – 341 = ____________ 341 – 272 = ____________

b. Does this pattern have a constant rate of change? Explain.

4. 112 56 28 14 7

Rule: ______________________

a. Find the difference between each pair of numbers in the pattern.

112 – 56 = ____________ 56 – 28 = ____________

28 – 14 = ____________ 14 – 7 = ____________

b. Does this pattern have a constant rate of change? Explain.

THINK

What can you say about patterns where the rule is to subtract the same number every time? What can you say about patterns where the rule is to divide by the same number every time?

Name ______________________ Date ___________

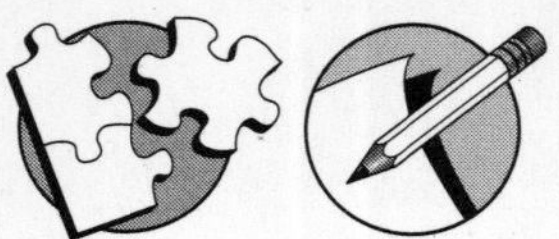

Patterns of Change

Find the change between each pair of numbers in the pattern. Find the pattern. Write the next three numbers in the pattern. Use words to describe the pattern.

1. 12 13 15 18 22 ________ ________ ________

+ 1 + 2 + 3 + 4

Pattern Description: ____

2. 6 8 14 22 36 ________ ________ ________

Pattern Description: ____

3. 88 78 69 61 54 ________ ________ ________

Pattern Description: ____

4. 119 105 93 83 75 ________ ________ ________

Pattern Description: ____

Name ____________________ Date __________

Patterns of Change (cont.)

5. 12 35 47 82 129 ______ ______ ______

Pattern Description: ______________________________

6. 13 14 17 22 29 ______ ______ ______

Pattern Description: ______________________________

7. 315 295 277 261 247 ______ ______ ______

Pattern Description: ______________________________

8. 7 11 18 29 47 ______ ______ ______

Pattern Description: ______________________________

DO MORE

Describe the different types of patterns used on these pages. How many types are there? How can you figure out what type of pattern is being used?

Name ______________________ Date ____________

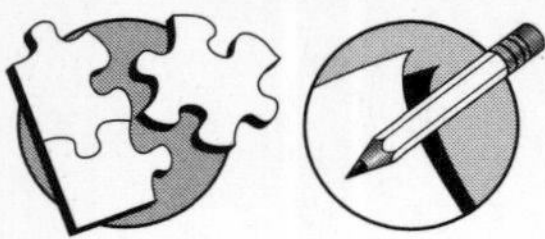

Functions Rule!

A **function machine** uses a rule to change numbers. Look for a pattern between the IN and OUT numbers in each table. Fill in the missing numbers. Write the rule.

1.

IN	5	19	21	6	13
OUT	15				39

Rule: ______________________

2.

IN	2	8	9	14	28
OUT		31	32		

Rule: ______________________

3.

IN	82	68	142	71	90
OUT		12			34

Rule: ______________________

4.

IN	64	100	92	124	16
OUT	16				4

Rule: ______________________

THINK

What method did you use to find the rules? Compare methods with a classmate.

0-7424-2885-0 *Using the Standards—Algebra*

Name ______________________ Date ____________

The Ins and Outs

A **function machine** uses a rule to change numbers. Look for a pattern between the IN and OUT numbers in each table. Fill in the missing numbers. Write the rule.

1.

IN		28	70			
OUT	6	19	61	33	26	5

Rule: ______________________

2.

IN		7			11	
OUT	28	49	56	98	77	42

Rule: ______________________

3.

IN	25	19			81	
OUT		1	4	56	63	15

Rule: ______________________

4.

IN	36	48		108	180	96
OUT		4	7	9		

Rule: ______________________

THINK

Use your rule to find the OUT number for each IN number. Do the answers match the information in the original table? If not, find your mistakes.

Name ______________________ Date ____________

Rule Reversal

The rule and the OUT values for each function machine are given below. Find the missing IN values.

1. Rule: OUT = IN + 52

IN					
OUT	79	132	85	60	108

2. Rule: OUT = IN − 19

IN					
OUT	12	35	80	66	27

3. Rule: OUT = IN x 13

IN					
OUT	39	104	130	65	52

4. Rule: OUT = IN ÷ 6

IN					
OUT	5	7	12	8	9

THINK

Explain how you found the missing IN values.

Name ______________________ Date ____________

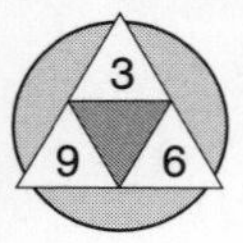

Word Power

Create a function machine to represent each situation. Tell what the IN and the OUT numbers mean. Write a rule for the function machine. Complete the IN/OUT tables. The first problem has been started for you.

1. Alexis has 40 more bracelets than Stephanie.

IN: number of bracelets Stephanie has

OUT: number of bracelets Alexis has

Rule: OUT = IN + 40

IN	0	4	16	31
OUT	40			

2. Miguel eats 15 fewer grapes than José.

IN: ______________________

OUT: ______________________

Rule: ______________________

IN	15	20	34	43
OUT				

3. Tarnell has three times as many fish as Deshawn.

IN: ______________________

OUT: ______________________

Rule: ______________________

IN	13	6	5	18
OUT				

4. Keidra got 11 more problems correct on the math test than Bobby.

IN: ______________________

OUT: ______________________

Rule: ______________________

IN	89	87	69	60
OUT				

DO MORE

A function machine has the rule OUT = IN – 25. Make up a situation that the function machine could represent. Use the function machine to create a table of IN and OUT numbers.

Name ______________________ Date ____________

It Takes Two

The following IN numbers will be put through two function machines. Each machine uses a different rule. The OUT values from the first machine become the IN values for the second machine. Find the rules for each machine.

1.

IN	7	11	13	15
OUT	12	16	18	20
IN	12	16	18	20
OUT	4	8	10	12

Rule 1: ______________________

Rule 2: ______________________

2.

IN	35	50	15	20	45
OUT	7	10	3	4	9
IN	7	10	3	4	9
OUT	11	14	7	8	13

Rule 1: ______________________

Rule 2: ______________________

3.

IN	3	6	7	8	10
OUT	27	54	63	72	90
IN	27	54	63	72	90
OUT	15	42	51	60	78

Rule 1: ______________________

Rule 2: ______________________

DO MORE

Create your own double function table. Choose a set of IN values. Choose 2 rules to use. See if someone else can find your rules.

Name ____________________ Date __________

Double Trouble

Function machines can represent real situations. Each situation below can be represented by two connected function machines. The OUT values from the first machine become the IN values for the second machine. Find the rule and the missing IN and OUT numbers for each function machine.

1. Julie watched twice as many movies as Carly this week. Andrea watched 5 fewer movies than Julie.

Carly **(IN)**	3	5	6	8	10
Julie **(OUT)**					

Rule: ____________________

Julie **(IN)**					
Andrea **(OUT)**					

Rule: ____________________

2. Gabriel made a dozen more cookies than Carlos. Tashon made half as many cookies as Gabriel.

Carlos **(IN)**	12	24	36	48	60
Gabriel **(OUT)**					

Rule: ____________________

Gabriel **(IN)**					
Tashon **(OUT)**					

Rule: ____________________

DO MORE

The rules for two function machines are OUT = IN x 4 and OUT = IN – 24. Make up a situation that the function machines could represent.

0-7424-2885-0 *Using the Standards—Algebra*

Name ______________________ Date ____________

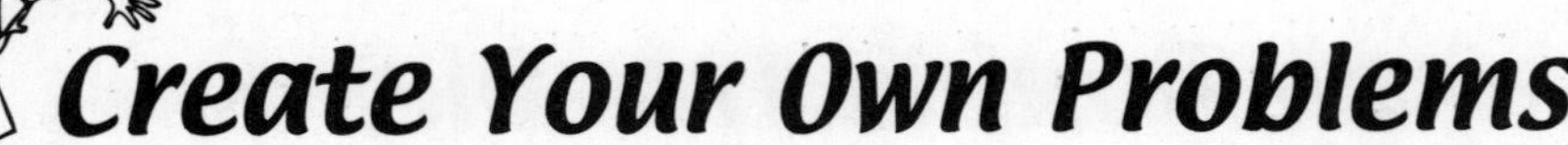

Create Your Own Problems

1. Create 3 repeating patterns using shapes, numbers, or movements. Each pattern should have the same letter pattern. Have a friend find the letter pattern that matches your repeating patterns.

2. Create a growing pattern and a decreasing pattern. Leave blank spaces in the patterns for a friend to fill in missing numbers. Have the friend describe the pattern or find a rule to fit the pattern.

3. Create two different growing patterns. Make one have a constant rate. See if a friend can find the patterns. Ask your friend which pattern has a constant rate.

4. Create a function machine with a certain rule. Make an IN and OUT table with some missing numbers. Ask a friend to find the rule and the missing IN and OUT numbers.

5. Make an IN and OUT table by using two function machines that follow a rule. See if your friend can find both rules.

6. Make up a situation and choose some IN numbers. Ask a friend to write the function machine rule that fits the situation and find the OUT numbers.

Name ____________________ Date __________

Check Your Skills

1. Fill in the missing numbers in the pattern. Identify the type of pattern (repeating, growing, or decreasing). Give a rule for the pattern.

a. 2 12 72 432 ____ ____ ____

Type: ____________ Rule: ____________

b. 99 87 75 63 ____ ____ ____

Type: ____________ Rule: ____________

c. 15 7 15 7 ____ ____ ____

Type: ____________ Rule: ____________

2. Find the next three numbers in each pattern. Describe each pattern. Which one(s) grow at a constant rate?

a. 4 6 10 16 24 ____________

b. 6 7 9 12 16 ____________

c. 12 20 28 36 44 ____________

3. A function machine uses a rule to change numbers. Look for a pattern between the IN and OUT numbers in the table. Fill in the missing numbers. Write the rule.

IN	13	25		39		72
OUT		75	48	117	66	216

Rule: ____________________

0-7424-2885-0 *Using the Standards—Algebra*

Name ______________________ Date __________

A Matter of Order

An operation is **commutative** if changing the order of the numbers does not change the answer.

Solve each arithmetic problem. Then change the order of the numbers and solve the new arithmetic problem. You may want to use a calculator. The first two problems have been started for you.

1. 1,721 + 589 = ________ 589 + 1,721 = ________

2. 876 − 245 = ________ 245 − 876 = ________

3. 75 − 43 = ________ ____________ = ________

4. 86 + 325 = ________ ____________ = ________

5. 782 − 543 = ________ ____________ = ________

6. 2,301 + 1,746 = ________ ____________ = ________

7. 658 + 702 = ________ ____________ = ________

8. 67 − 33 = ________ ____________ = ________

THINK

Is addition commutative? Is subtraction commutative? Explain how you know.

Name ______________________ Date ____________

A Short Commute

An operation is **commutative** if changing the order of the numbers does not change the answer.

Solve each arithmetic problem. Change the order of the numbers and solve the new arithmetic problem. You may want to use a calculator. The first two problems have been started for you.

1. 56 x 71 = __________ 71 x 56 = __________

2. 40 ÷ 8 = __________ 8 ÷ 40 = __________

3. 23 x 18 = __________ ______________ = __________

4. 180 ÷ 12 = __________ ______________ = __________

5. 66 ÷ 11 = __________ ______________ = __________

6. 13 x 45 = __________ ______________ = __________

7. 41 x 86 = __________ ______________ = __________

8. 384 ÷16 = __________ ______________ = __________

THINK

Is multiplication commutative? Is division commutative? Explain how you know.

Name ______________________ Date ___________

Awesome Associations

An operation is **associative** if changing the grouping does not change the answer.

A class was given the following addition problem. $(17 + 34) + 25$.
This is how Marissa solved it.

$17 + 34 = 51$
$51 + 25 = 76$

Eve chose to write the problem this way: $17 + (34 + 25)$.

1. Show how Eve would solve the problem.

2. What did Eve and Marissa do differently? Did they get the same answer?

Then the class was given the following subtraction problem. $52 - (36 - 15)$
This is how Marissa solved it.

$36 - 15 = 21$
$52 - 21 = 31$

Eve chose to write the problem this way: $(52 - 36) - 15$.

3. Show how Eve would solve the problem.

4. What did Eve and Marissa do differently? Did they get the same answer?

THINK

Do you think addition is associative? Do you think subtraction is associative? How could you prove your answers?

Name ______________________ Date __________

Great Groups

An operation is **associative** if changing the grouping does not change the answer.

A fifth-grade class was asked to solve the following multiplication problem. 18 x 4 x 21
Guillermo wrote and solved the problem this way. 18 x (4 x 21)
4 x 21 = 84
18 x 84 = 1,512

Miguel wrote the problem this way: (18 x 4) x 21.

1. Show how Miguel would solve the problem.

2. What did Miguel and Guillermo do differently? Did they get the same answer?

Then the class was given this problem. (18 ÷ 2) ÷ 3
This is how Guillermo solved the problem. 18 ÷ 2 = 9
9 ÷ 3 = 3

Miguel wrote the problem this way. 18 ÷ (2 ÷ 3)

3. Show how Miguel would solve the problem.

4. What did Miguel and Guillermo do differently? Did they get the same answer?

DO MORE

Do you think multiplication is associative? Do you think division is associative? How could you prove your answers?

Name ______________________ Date __________

To Commute or Not to Commute

An operation is **commutative** if changing the order of the numbers does not change the answer.

$$34 + 82 = 82 + 34$$

$$116 = 116$$

On which of the following problems can the commutative property be used? If the commutative property can be used, rewrite the problem. If not, write NA for not applicable.

1. $15 + 87$

2. $64 \div 4$

3. 33×56

4. $12 + 88$

5. 12×27

6. $15 \div 3$

7. $75 - 31$

8. $613 + 524$

9. $45 - 29$

DO MORE

Explain how you know whether or not the commutative property applies to each problem.

Name ____________________ Date __________

With Whom to Associate?

An operation is **associative** if changing the grouping does not change the answer.

$$3 \times (5 \times 6) = (3 \times 5) \times 6$$

$$3 \times 30 = 15 \times 6$$

$$90 = 90$$

On which of the following problems can the associative property be used? If the associative property can be used, rewrite the problem. If not, write NA for not applicable.

1. $(56 - 32) - 15$
2. $48 \div (12 \div 6)$
3. $251 + (88 + 31)$
4. $(4 \times 15) \times 8$
5. $(22 + 76) + 91$
6. $3 \times (14 \times 5)$
7. $(12 \times 7) \times 2$
8. $415 + (88 + 21)$
9. $(100 \div 50) \div 5$

DO MORE

Explain how you know whether or not the commutative property applies to each problem.

Name ____________________ Date __________

Proper Properties

Find the sum of each list of numbers. To make it easier, use the commutative and associative properties to change the order and regroup the numbers into sums of 10. Write down the name of the property when you use it.

Example: $7 + 9 + 3 + 5 + 6 + 8 + 4 + 9 + 2 + 1$
$= 7 + 3 + 9 + 1 + 8 + 2 + 6 + 4 + 9 + 5$ commutative property
$= (7 + 3) + (9 + 1) + (8 + 2) + (6 + 4) + (9 + 5)$ associative property
$= 10 + 10 + 10 + 10 + 14$
$= 40 + 14$
$= 54$

1. $9 + 7 + 6 + 3 + 8 + 4 + 1$

2. $8 + 6 + 5 + 3 + 4 + 7 + 2 + 5$

3. $6 + 3 + 2 + 6 + 7 + 4$

4. $1 + 6 + 5 + 3 + 7 + 4 + 5$

5. $1 + 8 + 3 + 6 + 5 + 4 + 2 + 7 + 9 + 5$

6. $7 + 9 + 3 + 5 + 1 + 6 + 8 + 4 + 5$

THINK

In what other ways could the commutative and associative properties be useful?

Name ______________________ Date __________

Perplexing Properties

An operation is **commutative** if changing the order of the numbers does not change the answer.

$$34 + 82 = 82 + 34$$
$$116 = 116$$

An operation is **associative** if changing the grouping does not change the answer.

$$3 + (5 + 6) = (3 + 5) + 6$$
$$3 + 11 = 8 + 6$$
$$14 = 14$$

Rewrite each expression in an equivalent form using the commutative or associative property. Write commutative or associative to show which property was used.

1. $(54 + 15) + 25 =$ ________________ ________________

2. $17 \times 12 =$ ________________ ________________

3. $85 + 66 =$ ________________ ________________

4. $3 \times (24 \times 5) =$ ________________ ________________

5. $(412 + 180) + (79 + 366) =$ ________________ ________________

6. $62 \times (8 \times 14) =$ ________________ ________________

DO MORE

How can you prove that the expressions you wrote are equivalent to the original?

Name ______________________ Date ____________

Multiplication Models

Trevor drew the model below to represent the expression 3 x 6 + 3 x 5.

3 x 6 + 3 x 5

1. What part of the expression represents the number of white circles? ____________

2. How many white circles are there? ____________

3. What part of the expression represents the number of shaded circles? ____________

4. How many shaded circles are there? ____________

5. How many total circles are there? ____________

6. Compute the answer using arithmetic. Does your answer match the total number of circles in the model? ____________

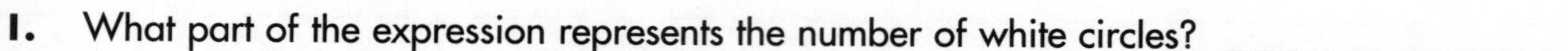

Name _______________________ Date ___________

Multiplication Models (cont.)

Layanna had an idea for another way to solve this problem. She drew the following model and wrote this expression.

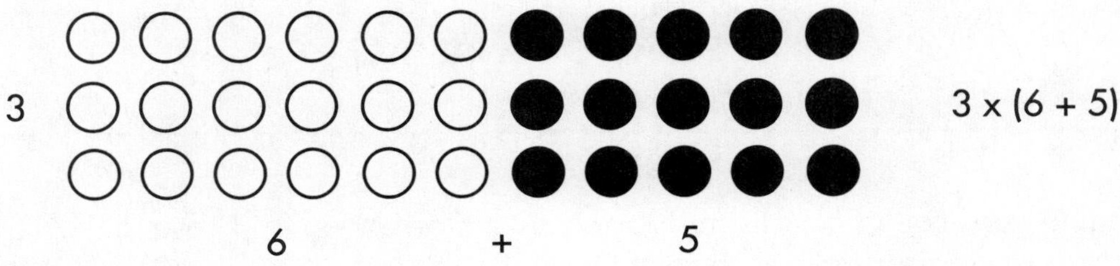

7. Compare Trevor's model to Layanna's model. What do you notice?

8. What does the (6 + 5) in Layanna's expression represent on the model?

9. Why does multiplying 3 by (6 + 5) find the total number of circless in the model?

10. Does Layanna's method give the same answer as Trevor's method? Why or why not?

THINK

The **distributive property** says that if you have any three numbers, A, B, and C, then A x B + A x C = A x (B + C). How does this property relate to the models Trevor and Layanna drew?

Name ______________________ Date __________

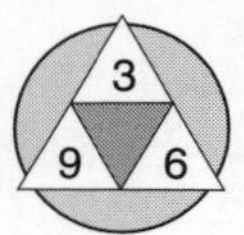

Trading Cards

The **distributive property** says that if you have any three numbers, A, B, and C, then

$$A \times B + A \times C = A \times (B + C).$$

Luke has a trading card collection. His football cards are arranged in 4 rows of 7. His baseball cards are arranged in 4 rows of 9.

1. Draw a model of Luke's trading card collection.

2. Write an expression that represents this model. ______________________

3. How many total trading cards does Luke have? Show your work.

4. Luke mixes his trading cards together and lays them out in rows of four. Draw a model of Luke's trading card collection now.

5. How many cards will be in each row? ______________________

6. Write an expression to represent this model. ______________________

7. How many trading cards does Luke have now? Show your work.

8. Explain how the models you drew are related to the distributive property.

DO MORE

Katya has 4 boxes. Each box contains 3 shells. Katya has 4 more boxes, each containing 7 stones. If Katya combines the stones and shells into only 4 boxes, how many items would be in each box?

Name ____________________ Date __________

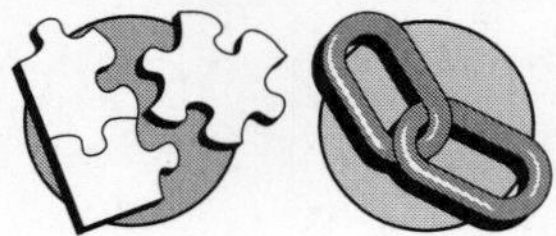

Daring Distributions

The **distributive property** says that if you have any three numbers, A, B, and C, then

$$A \times B + A \times C = A \times (B + C).$$

Solve each problem. Write an equation that shows how the distributive property applies to each situation. You may want to draw a picture or use counters to model the problems.

1. Charles bought 4 bags of candy with 12 chocolates each and 4 bags with 5 peppermints each. Charles plans to split the candy evenly among 4 boys. How many pieces of candy will each boy receive?

2. Keisha just bought some smelly stickers and sparkly stickers. The smelly stickers come in a pack of 2 sheets with 4 stickers per sheet. The sparkly stickers come in a pack of 2 sheets with 6 stickers per sheet. Keisha places her stickers in an album. She arranges them in 2 columns. How many stickers will be in each column? How many stickers does she have all together?

3. Jawon is making chocolate-chip cookies. He has 2 baking sheets. On one baking sheet, there is room for 3 rows of 4 cookies. On the other baking sheet, there is room for 3 rows of 5 cookies. When the cookies are done, Jawon places them on waxed paper. He places them in 3 rows. How many cookies are in each row? How many cookies did he bake in all?

4. Miguelita loves to read. She has two bookshelves. One has 5 shelves with 15 hardcover books on each shelf. The second shelf has 5 shelves with 25 paperback books on each shelf. When her family moved, she evenly distributed her books into 5 boxes. How many books were in each box? How many total books does she have?

THINK

Six groups of 5 plus 6 groups of 4 is the same as 6 groups of 9. Do you agree or disagree with this statement? Why?

Name ______________________ Date __________

Multiplication Made Easy

The **distributive property** says that if you have any three numbers, A, B, and C, then

$$B \times A + C \times A = (B + C) \times A.$$

Olivia is trying to solve the following multiplication problem: 56 x 9.

She decides to break the problem down to make it easier.

First, she puts 56 into expanded form.	56 = 50 + 6
So, her problem now looks like this.	(50 + 6) x 9
She uses the distributive property.	50 x 9 + 6 x 9
She performs the multiplication in her head.	450 + 54
She finds the sum.	504

Solve the following multiplication problems using Olivia's break-down method. Show your work.

1. 88 x 5

2. 54 x 3

3. 38 x 7

4. 81 x 2

Name ______________________ Date ____________

Multiplication Made Easy (cont.)

5. 44 x 9

6. 67 x 6

7. 78 x 8

8. 99 x 5

9. 33 x 12

10. 143 x 5

11. 325 x 8

12. 83 x 11

13. 643 x 4

14. 309 x 3

DO MORE

Check your answers by using a different method to multiply.

Name ______________________ Date ____________

Diligent Digits

In each of the following puzzles, each letter stands for a different digit between 0 and 9. Some of the digits are known. Use these to help you find the other digits that make the addition and multiplication problems true.

1.

```
  a b c b
+   a d c
---------
  d e d b
```

a = ______ b = ______ c = ______
d = 8 e = 6

2.

```
  a b b c
+   g d c
---------
  a e f f
```

a = 3 b = ______ c = 6 d = ______
e = 5 f = ______ g = ______

3.

```
  a b c d
+ e f f g
---------
  h e i j
```

a = 1 b = ______ c = ______ d = 4
e = ______ f = ______ g = ______ h = 8
i = 9 j = 0

4.

```
   a b c
x      d
--------
 f f c e
```

a = 3 b = ______ c = ______
d = 6 e = 0 f = ______

5.

```
   a b b
x      c
--------
 a e c d
```

a = ______ b = ______ c = 9
d = 3 e = 1

DO MORE

Make your own puzzle. See if a friend can solve it. Does your puzzle have more than one right answer?

0-7424-2885-0 *Using the Standards—Algebra*

Name ______________________ Date __________

Name That Digit!

Each letter represents a different digit between 0 and 9. Read the clues about each number to find its digits.

1. a, b c d

Clue: I am a 4-digit, odd number between 7,000 and 8,000. The sum of my first 2 digits is 15. The sum of my last 2 digits is 15. Find my digits.

a = _____ b = _____ c = _____ d = _____

2. e, f g h

Clue: I am a 4-digit number greater than 3,100. The sum of my digits is 6. I am divisible by 4.

e = _____ f = _____ g = _____ h = _____

3. a b, b c d

Clue: I am a 5-digit number less than 40,000. The sum of my first 2 digits is 6. The sum of my last 3 digits is 11. My ones digit is twice as large as my tens digit.

a = _____ b = _____ c = _____ d = _____

4. e f, e g f

Clue: I am a 5-digit number. The sum of my first 2 digits is 9. The sum of my last 3 digits is 10. My ones digit is 1 greater than my tens digit.

e = _____ f = _____ g = _____

THINK

Compare problem-solving strategies with a classmate.

0-7424-2885-0 *Using the Standards—Algebra*

Name ______________________ Date __________

Fruit Salad

> A **variable** is a letter or symbol that stands for an unknown number.

Each fruit symbol below represents a different number. Some of the numbers are known, but others are a mystery. Use the equations to help find the mystery numbers.

= 25 = 17 = 4

– =

– =

x =

÷ =

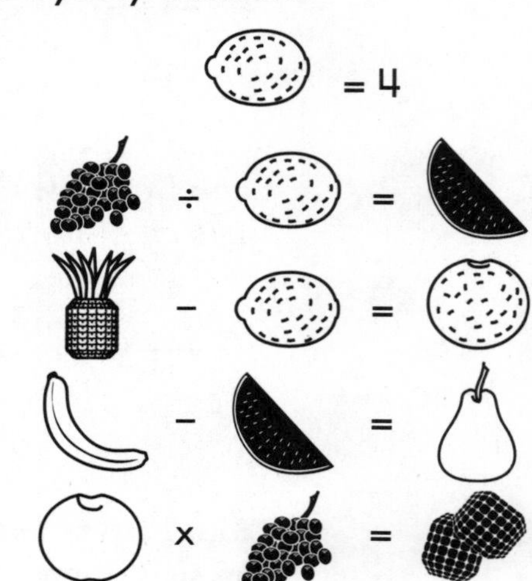

1. = _____
2. = _____
3. = _____
4. = _____
5. = _____
6. = _____
7. = _____
8. = _____

DO MORE

Use these symbols to make up your own equations. Make up your own symbols to represent other numbers. See if a friend can find your mystery numbers.

Name ______________________ Date ___________

Crack the Code

Crack the code to find the secret phrase. Each letter stands for a different number. Use the clues to find out which number each letter represents. Then place the correct letter above the number it represents at the bottom of the page.

Clues:

C = 10	A is $\frac{1}{2}$ of C.	E is 9 more than A.
I is twice the value of E.	O is C less than I.	T is equal to I ÷ 7.
N is 3 times greater than A.	L is T more than N.	G is equal to A x T.
H is $\frac{1}{4}$ of I.	S is H more than G.	Y is equal to S – E.

___ ___ ___ ___ ___ ___   ___ ___   ___ ___ ___

10 7 5 15 20 14   28 27   4 7 14

___ ___ ___ ___   ___ ___ ___ ___ ___ ___ ___ ___

18 15 19 13   10 18 15 27 4 5 15 4

DO MORE

Make up your own secret phrase. Choose numbers to represent each letter. Make up some clues. Write your phrase in code using the numbers. Ask a friend to use your clues to crack the code.

Name ____________________ Date __________

Simple Symbols

A **variable** is a letter or symbol that stands for an unknown number.

Use the inverse operation to find the value of each variable. The first few problems have been started for you.

1. 231 + ♡ = 750

750 – 231 = ♡

♡ = __________

2. 🕷 ÷ 13 = 32

32 x 13 = 🕷

🕷 = __________

3. ☘ x 17 = 153

153 ÷ 17 = ☘

☘ = __________

4. 🍌 – 642 = 1,328

🍌 = __________

5. ☾ + 273 = 1,110

☾ = __________

6. 676 – ◇ = 459

◇ = __________

7. 🍓 x 23 = 345

🍓 = __________

8. ✿ ÷ 48 = 12

✿ = __________

DO MORE

Create your own equations with a variable. See if a classmate can find the value of the variables.

Name ______________________ Date __________

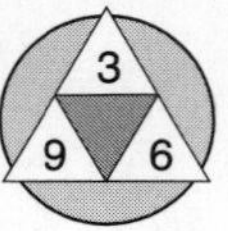

Vintage Variables

A **variable** is a letter or symbol that stands for an unknown number.

Find the value of each variable that makes the equation true.

1. $5{,}153 + T = 775$

   $T =$ __________

2. $M \div 32 = 43$

   $M =$ __________

3. $71 \times K = 1{,}278$

   $K =$ __________

4. $P - 688 = 735$

   $P =$ __________

5. $S + 583 = 6{,}302$

   $S =$ __________

6. $62{,}576 - R = 31{,}552$

   $R =$ __________

7. $N \div 62 = 44$

   $N =$ __________

8. $V \times 45 = 405$

   $V =$ __________

THINK

Explain the strategies you used to find the value of each variable.

Name ______________________ Date ____________

Doing the Two-Step

A **variable** is a letter or symbol that stands for an unknown number.

Use the equations to find the value of each variable.

1. $3 \times N + 4 = 25$

$N =$ ________

2. $6 = 108 \div M$

$M =$ ________

3. $12 \times P - 55 = 53$

$P =$ ________

4. $Q \div 8 + 24 = 30$

$Q =$ ________

5. $17 + 5 \times R = 42$

$R =$ ________

6. $S \div 12 + 8 = 23$

$S =$ ________

THINK

Explain how you solved each equation. What strategies did you use?

Name ______________________ Date __________

Two Is Company

A **variable** is a letter or symbol that stands for an unknown number. If there are two variables in an equation, there are many different pairs of numbers that make the equation true.

Example: $t - v = 12$
$20 - 8 = 12$
$15 - 3 = 12$
$22 - 10 = 12$

t	v
20	8
15	3
22	10

For each equation, find the missing number that completes each pair.

1. $b \times 3 = c$

b	c
5	
	45
8	
	108

2. $d - 110 = e$

d	e
200	
	70
563	
	335

3. $f + g = 528$

f	g
271	
	466
319	
	25

4. $240 \div h = j$

h	j
6	
	6
4	
	10

DO MORE

For each equation above, find another pair that makes the equation true.

Name ______________________ Date ____________

Duo Delight

In each problem, different symbols stand for different numbers. Find the numbers that will make both equations true.

1. + = 30

+ 6 =

= ______ = ______

2. 180 ÷ =

+ = 36

= ______ = ______

3. 47 − =

+ 13 = 28

= ______ = ______

4. − = 20

x = 125

= ______ = ______

5. − = 255

÷ 3 = 120

= ______ = ______

6. x = 96

− = 4

= ______ = ______

7. 256 ÷ = 32

x = 104

= ______ = ______

8. + = 41

− = 19

= ______ = ______

DO MORE

How can you prove that your answers are correct?

0-7424-2885-0 *Using the Standards—Algebra*

Name ____________________ Date __________

Triple Triumph

For each problem below, different shapes represent different numbers. Find the numbers for each shape that make all three equations true.

1. [hexagon] + [hexagon] = 168   [triangle] x 3 = [rectangle]   [rectangle] − [hexagon] = 39

[hexagon] = ________   [triangle] = ________   [rectangle] = ________

2. [parallelogram] + [trapezoid] + [kite] = 73   [parallelogram] x [trapezoid] = 300   [parallelogram] + 76 = 88

[parallelogram] = ________   [trapezoid] = ________   [kite] = ________

3. [pentagon] x 12 = [square]   [square] − [circle] = 179   196 ÷ [pentagon] = 7

[pentagon] = ________   [square] = ________   [circle] = ________

4. [oval] − [octagon] = 16   [oval] x 5 = [right triangle]   [oval] x [octagon] = 36

[oval] = ________   [octagon] = ________   [right triangle] = ________

DO MORE

Find a partner. Compare the strategies you used to solve these problems.

Name ________________________ Date ____________

Canned Food Drive

Crystal Lake Elementary School is sponsoring a canned-food drive. Use the clues to find out how many cans each class or grade collected.

G = Mr. Garcia's class	*C* = Ms. Carson's class	*J* = Ms. Jackson's class
F = Fifth-grade classes	*T* = Third-grade classes	*S* = Second-grade classes
R = Ms. Rodriguez's class	*D* = Ms. Daniel's class	*H* = Mr. Herrera's class
I = First-grade classes	*K* = Kindergarten classes	*P* = Preschool classes

1. The fourth-grade classes brought a total of 320 cans. Mr. Garcia's class brought 20 more cans than Ms. Carson's class. Ms. Jackson's class alone brought in half of the total amount.

G = __________ *C* = __________ *J* = __________

2. The fifth-grade classes collected 25% more cans than the fourth-grade classes. This was twice as many cans as the second and third-grade classes combined. The second-grade class collected 50 more cans than the third-grade class.

S = __________ *T* = __________ *F* = __________

3. The first-grade classes collected 40 fewer cans than the fourth-grade classes. Ms. Rodriguez's class brought in 30% of the first-grade total. Mr. Herrera's class brought in 50% of the first-grade total and Ms. Daniel's class brought in the rest of the first-grade cans.

I = __________ *R* = __________ *H* = __________ *D* = __________

4. The kindergarten classes collected 20% fewer cans than the fourth-grade classes. The preschool classes collected 40 fewer cans than the kindergarten classes.

K = __________ *P* = __________

THINK

How do you know your answers are correct?

Name ______________________ Date __________

Something's Fishy

The Something's Fishy store sells all kinds of aquarium fish. They are taking inventory. Use the clues to find out how many of each type of fish the store owns.

A = Angels	B = Bettas	C = Clowns
T = Tetras	G = Goldfish	D = Danios
H = Cichlids	P = Plecos	M = Mollys
S = Swordtails	R = Gouramis	N = Tangs

1. There are a total of 200 Mollys, Tangs, and Bettas. There are half as many Tangs as Mollys. There are 25 more Bettas than Mollys.

   N = __________ B = __________ M = __________

2. There are 25 Plecos. There are twice as many Tetras as there are Plecos and Angels combined. There are 20% more Angel fish than Plecos.

   P = __________ A = __________ T = __________

3. There are 8 times as many Clown fish as Gouramis. There are 70 fewer Danios than there are Clown fish. There are 250 Clowns and Danios combined.

   R = __________ C = __________ D = __________

4. There are a total of 490 Goldfish, Cichlids, and Swordtails. There are twice as many Goldfish as Cichlids. There are half as many Swordtails as Cichlids.

   G = __________ H = __________ S = __________

THINK

How do you know your answers are correct?

Name ______________________ Date ____________

Have a Ball!

A **variable** is a letter or symbol that stands for an unknown number. If there are two variables in an equation, there are many different pairs of numbers that make the equation true.

1. Hunter and Damarius like to play soccer. Last year, Damarius made 9 more goals than Hunter did. Hunter made H goals and Damarius made D goals.

a. Write an equation showing this relationship.

____

b. Complete the following table showing the number of goals each boy scored.

H	D
12	
20	
	18
	26

2. Dayani and Carlita played a game of one-on-one basketball. Carlita made 12 fewer shots than Dayani. Dayani made D baskets and Carlita made C baskets.

a. Write an equation showing this relationship.

____

b. Complete the following table showing the number of baskets each girl scored.

C	D
8	
12	
	30
	42

DO MORE

For each of the problems, find three more pairs of numbers that would work in the equations. Tell what the numbers mean in that situation.

Name ______________________ Date ____________

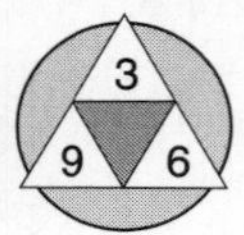

Field Trip

A **variable** is a letter or symbol that stands for an unknown number. If there are two variables in an equation, there are many different pairs of numbers that make the equation true.

1. The fifth-grade class is going on a field trip. There are *S* students going on the trip. The trip costs $5 per person. *T* is the total cost of the trip for the whole class.

a. Write an equation showing the relationship between *S* and *T*.

____

b. Complete the following table showing the total cost of the trip depending on how many students sign up.

S	*T*
52	
60	
	175
	240

2. On the fifth-grade field trip, each bus is full and holds 28 people. There are *B* buses and *P* people on the trip.

a. Write an equation showing the relationship between *B* and *P*.

____

b. Complete the following table showing the number of buses needed based on the number of people going on the trip.

P	*B*
56	
84	
112	
140	

DO MORE

For each of the problems, find three more pairs of numbers that would work in the equations. Tell what the numbers mean in that situation.

0-7424-2885-0 *Using the Standards—Algebra*

Name ____________________ Date __________

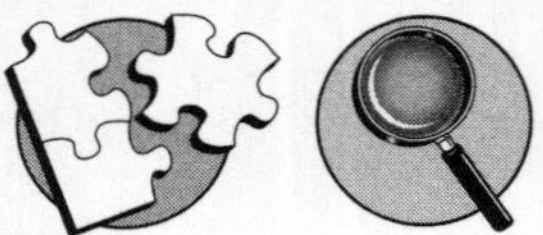

Phone Fright

Equations are often used to help solve problems.
A **variable** is a letter that represents the amount you are trying to find.

Follow the steps to help solve this word problem:

The Chord Free cellular telephone company charges $35 a month for service. They offer unlimited weekends and evenings, but charge $0.15 a minute for calls at any other time. This month, Jenna had a bill for $69.95. How many minutes did she spend talking during weekdays this month?

1. Use words to write an equation describing the relationship between the known and unknown values in the problem.

2. Choose a variable for this problem. Tell what the variable represents. ______________

3. Replace the words in the sentence with numbers and variables to make a mathematical equation.

4. Solve the equation you wrote in problem 3. Show how you found your answer.

5. Write the answer to the problem in a complete sentence.

DO MORE

How can you show that your final answer is correct?

0-7424-2885-0 *Using the Standards—Algebra*

Name ______________________ Date ____________

Credit Catastrophe

Equations are often used to help solve problems.
A **variable** is a letter that represents the amount you are trying to find.

Follow the steps to help solve this word problem:

Isaac has a charge card that charges 15% interest on his unpaid balance. Isaac charged a $150 stereo on his credit card. He paid a minimum charge of $25 this month. How much will his balance be next month?

1. Use words to write an equation describing the relationship between the known and unknown values in the problem.

2. Choose a variable for this problem. Tell what the variable represents. ______________

3. Replace the words in the sentence with numbers and variables to make a mathematical equation.

4. Solve the equation you wrote in problem 3. Show how you found your answer.

5. Write the answer to the question in a complete sentence.

DO MORE

How can you show that your answer is correct?

0-7424-2885-0 *Using the Standards—Algebra*

Name ______________________ Date ____________

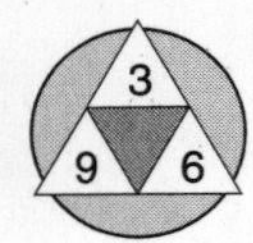

Choice Words

Equations are often used to help solve problems.
A **variable** is a letter that represents an unknown amount.

For each word problem, choose a letter to use for a variable and tell what the variable represents. Then write an equation that models the problem. Solve the problem, show your work, and answer the question in a complete sentence.

1. Mei is a library aid. She is shelving books. There are a total of 788 books. Some of the books will be displayed on a table. The rest will be placed on 6 bookshelves, each of which holds 128 books. If the bookshelves are all filled, how many books will be displayed on the table?

2. Jared's family rented a mini-van for a trip. The rental company charges $15 plus $0.25 for each mile traveled. If the family paid a total of $90, how many miles did they travel?

3. Caitlin works at a retail store. She makes $6 an hour. But, $25 will be taken from her first paycheck to pay for her uniform. If she gets a $95 check her first week, how many hours did she work?

Name ______________________ Date __________

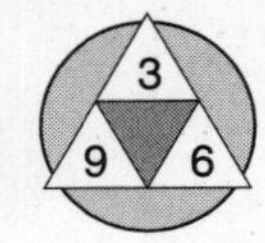

Choice Words (cont.)

4. There are 100 people at a sports banquet. Each table at the banquet holds 7 people. But, there are 2 people who do not have seats! How many tables were set up?

5. A sweater normally costs $50. It's on sale for 25% off. How much is the discount on the sweater?

6. A new mountain bike sells for $250. Alegria bought the bike on sale for $100 less than the retail price. What percentage discount did she get?

7. Bobby purchases $22 worth of trading cards. The sales tax in his state is 8%. How much is the tax on his purchase?

8. Deshawn collects comic books. He keeps them in protective plastic sleeves in boxes. He has 491 comic books. A full box holds 30 comics. All of his boxes are full, except for one, which has 11 comics in it. How many full boxes does he have?

THINK

How can writing equations help you solve problems?

Name ______________________ Date __________

In the Fast Lane

Caroline and her little sister Miranda are racing go carts on a track. Caroline gives her sister a 60 meter head start. The following tables show how far each girl has traveled at each minute of the race.

Caroline

Time (minutes)	Distance (meters)
0	0
1	281
2	562
3	843
4	1,124
5	1,405
6	1,686

Miranda

Time (minutes)	Distance (meters)
0	60
1	328
2	596
3	864
4	1,132
5	1,400
6	1,668

1. How fast was Caroline traveling each minute? How do you know?

2. How fast was Miranda traveling each minute? How do you know?

0-7424-2885-0 *Using the Standards—Algebra*

Name ______________________ Date __________

In the Fast Lane (cont.)

3. Write an equation showing the relationship between time and Caroline's distance from the starting line.

4. Write an equation showing the relationship between the time and Miranda's distance from the starting line.

5. How can you test to make sure the equations you wrote accurately model the race?

6. If the race was 800 meters long, who would win?

If the race was 1,500 meters long, who would win?

DO MORE

Explain how equations can be useful for modeling real-life situations.

Name ______________________ Date ____________

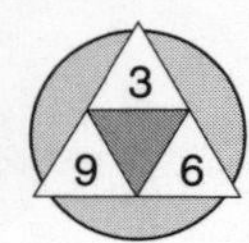

Utterly Unknown

Equations are often used to help solve problems.
A **variable** is a letter that represents an unknown amount.

1. Danny's father is repairing the roof of their house. The U-Break-It-U-Buy-It rental company charges \$35 a day plus a \$3 processing fee to rent an air-powered nail gun. Danny's father paid \$143 when he returned the nail gun. How many days did he have it?

a. Choose (a) variable(s) to represent any unknown amounts. Tell what the variable represents.

b. Write an equation that will help you solve this problem. Solve the equation.

c. Write your answer to the problem in a complete sentence.

2. Lakisha likes to make scrapbooks. She has both photo pages and journal pages in her scrapbook. She has J journal pages and P photo pages.

a. There are a total of 112 pages in Lakisha's scrapbook. Write an equation showing the relationship between journal pages and photo pages. ______________________

b. There are 58 more photo pages than there are journal pages in her scrapbook. Write an equation showing this relationship. ______________________

c. How many journal pages and photo pages does Lakisha have in her scrapbook? Show your work.

$J =$ __________ $P =$ __________

0-7424-2885-0 *Using the Standards—Algebra*

Name ______________________ Date ____________

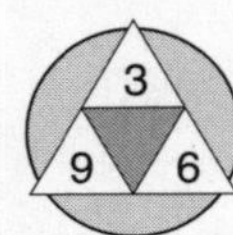

Utterly Unknown (cont.)

3. Dante decided to make some money raking lawns. He charges $7 per lawn. In September he made *S* dollars and in October he made *O* dollars.

- **a.** He made a total of $259 for those 2 months. Write an equation showing this relationship. ______________________
- **b.** He made $49 more in October than he did in September. Write an equation showing this relationship. ______________________
- **c.** How much money did Dante make each month? Show your work.

  O = __________ *S* = __________

- **d.** Write 2 equations showing the relationship between the number of lawns he raked, *L*, in a month, and the amount of money he earned each month. __________
- **e.** How many lawns did Dante rake in September? __________ In October? __________

4. Adelina is selling cookies at the school bake sale. She sold *C* chocolate chip cookies, *S* sugar cookies, and *P* peanut butter cookies.

- **a.** She sold 4 dozen chocolate chip and sugar cookies combined. Write an equation showing this relationship. ______________________
- **b.** She sold twice as many chocolate chip cookies as she did peanut butter cookies. Write an equation showing this relationship. ______________________
- **c.** She sold one dozen more chocolate chip cookies than sugar cookies. Write an equation showing this relationship. ______________________
- **d.** How many of each type of cookie did she sell? Tell how you found your answers.

  C = __________ *S* = __________ *P* = __________

THINK

If you have only one variable, how many equations do you need to have in order to find its value? If you have 2 variables, how many equations do you need? What if you have 3 variables?

Name ______________________ Date __________

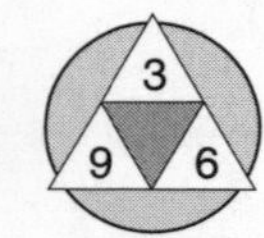

Bargain Days

Equations are often used to help solve problems. A **variable** is a letter that represents the amount you are trying to find. Follow the steps to help solve this word problem.

Blake has $50 of birthday money to spend. A skateboard that he wants is normally priced at $70, but is on sale for 35% off. Sales tax in his state is 6%. Does Blake have enough money to buy the skateboard?

1. Before Blake can answer the question, he has to calculate the discount, the price of the skateboard, the sales tax, and the total cost of his purchase. The following word equation can help you begin to solve this problem. Choose a variable to use for the unknown amount. Tell what the variable means. Replace the words with numbers or variables to create a mathematical equation.

   Discount = percentage as a decimal x original amount

2. Solve the equation and find the value of the variable. Show your work.

3. Write a word equation that describes how to find the sale price of the skateboard.

   Sale Price = ______________________________

4. Choose a variable to use for the unknown amount. Tell what the variable means. Replace the words in problem 3 with numbers or variables to create a mathematical equation.

5. Solve the equation and find the value of the variable. Show your work.

6. Write a word equation that describes how to find the amount of sales tax.

   Tax = ______________________________

Name ______________________ Date __________

Bargain Days (cont.)

7. Choose a variable to use for the unknown amount. Tell what the variable means. Replace the words in problem 6 with numbers or variables to create a mathematical equation.

8. Solve the equation and find the value of the variable. Show your work.

9. Write a word equation that describes how to find the total cost of the skateboard, including tax.

   Total Cost = ______________________________

10. Choose a variable to use for the unknown amount. Tell what the variable means. Replace the words in problem 6 with numbers or variables to create a mathematical equation.

11. Solve the equation and find the value of the variable. Show your work.

12. Write your final answer in a complete sentence.

THINK

Describe the strategies you can use to solve a problem with multiple steps.

Name ______________________ Date ____________

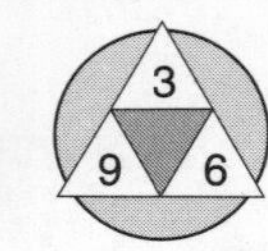

It's a Gas, Gas, Gas!

Equations are often used to help solve problems. A **variable** is a letter that represents the amount you are trying to find. Follow the steps to help solve this word problem.

Starting with a full 15-gallon tank, Cheyenne traveled for 360 miles before stopping for gas. She added 12 gallons of gas to fill the tank. She has another 500 miles to travel. Will she need to stop for gas again?

1. In order to answer the question you need to know how far the car can travel on 15 gallons of gas (a full tank). To find this, you first need to know how far the car can travel on 1 gallon. This is called the gas mileage. Use M as the variable in this problem. What should M represent?

   M = ____

2. The following word equation can help you solve this problem. Replace the words with numbers or variables to create a mathematical equation.

   # of gallons used x mileage per gallon = total # of miles traveled

3. Find the value of M that makes this equation true. Show how you found your answer.

4. Now you can find the answer to the question. Use the same word equation to write a different mathematical equation. Choose a variable and tell what it means.

5. Solve your equation. Show how you found your answer.

6. Write your final answer in complete sentences.

THINK

How can writing a word equation help you solve the problem?

0-7424-2885-0 *Using the Standards—Algebra*

Name ________________________ Date ____________

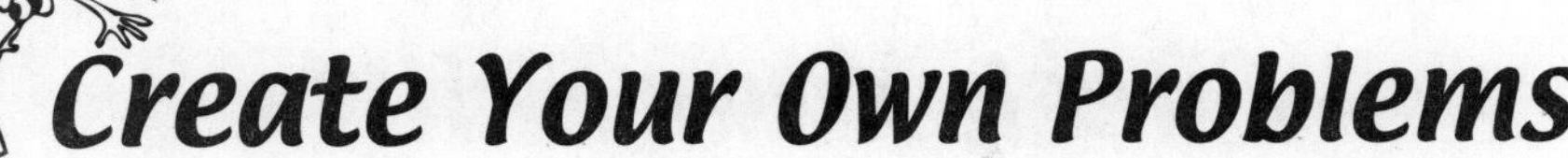

Create Your Own Problems

1. Write 3 different addition or multiplication equations. Then rewrite each equation using the commutative or associative property. Ask a classmate to figure out which property was used to rewrite the equation.

2. Write 4 equations: one with addition, one with subtraction, one with multiplication, and one with division. Each equation should have one unknown value. Use a different symbol to represent each unknown value. Have a classmate solve your equations.

3. Choose two numbers between 2 and 10. Find their product and then find their sum. Now, choose a different symbol to represent each of the numbers. Use the product and sum to write two equations using the symbols. See if a classmate can use the equations to find your two numbers.

4. Make up a story problem with two unknown amounts. Tell how the amounts are related to each other. Choose a letter to represent each variable. Have a classmate write an equation that models the problem. Give an amount for one of the variables and have your classmate find the value of the other variable.

5. Make up a story problem involving percentages.

Name ____________________ Date ____________

Check Your Skills

1. Use the commutative, associative, or distributive property to rewrite each equation in an equivalent form. Tell which property you used.

a. (17 + 92) + 12 = ____________ ____________

b. 5 x (50 + 62) = ____________ ____________

c. 33 x 16 = ____________ ____________

2. I am an odd 4-digit number greater than 2,000. The sum of my digits is 14. The hundreds digit is less than the ones digit. The tens digit is 3 times greater than the thousands digit. What number am I? ____________

3. Each symbol stands for a different number. Find the number that makes each equation true.

a. 5,721 + ☘ = 7,062

☘ = ____________

b. 18 x ☾ + 16 = 106

☾ = ____________

c. 192 ÷ ☆ − 8 = 4

☆ = ____________

d. 930 ÷ ◇ = 31

◇ = ____________

4. Gwen is bringing candy to school for a class party. She brought a total of 95 pieces of licorice, chocolate, and hard candy. She brought twice as many pieces of licorice as hard candy. She brought fifteen fewer pieces of hard candy than chocolate. There were 75 pieces of licorice and chocolate combined. How many pieces of each type did she bring?

L = ____________ *C* = ____________ *H* = ____________

5. Each letter stands for a number. Find the numbers that make both equations true.

a. $B - D = 7$

$B \times D = 60$

B = ____________

D = ____________

b. $R + T = 21$

$98 \div T = R$

R = ____________

T = ____________

0-7424-2885-0 Using the Standards—Algebra

Name ______________________ Date ____________

Check Your Skills (cont.)

6. Rashon decides to make some money by babysitting. He borrows $25 from his dad to take an infant and child CPR class. He plans to charge $6 an hour for babysitting.

a. Let H represent the number of hours he works the first month. Let P represent his profit. Write an equation showing the relationship between P and H. ____________________

b. If Rashon works 40 hours, what will be his total profit?

$H =$ __________ $P =$ __________

c. If Rashon made a profit of $125, how many hours did he work?

$H =$ __________ $P =$ __________

7. Erin wants to buy a new special-edition DVD that will be released soon. The retail price is $45. But, if she preorders it she can save 5% on the cost. How much will the DVD cost?

a. Choose a variable to represent the unknown amount and write an equation that models this problem.

b. Solve the equation. Show your work.

c. Answer the question in a complete sentence.

8. Jim goes to the store and buys a computer game that costs $25 and a jacket that costs $40, but is on sale for 20% off. The sales tax in his state is 8%. What is the total cost, including tax, of his purchases? Use variables and equations to show you got your answer.

Name ______________________ Date ___________

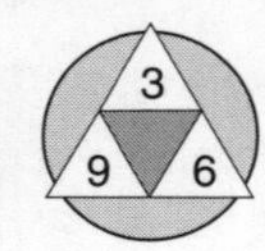

Building Basics

Materials: unit cubes

This is a scale drawing of an office building that is being planned. Use unit cubes to build a scale model of the building.

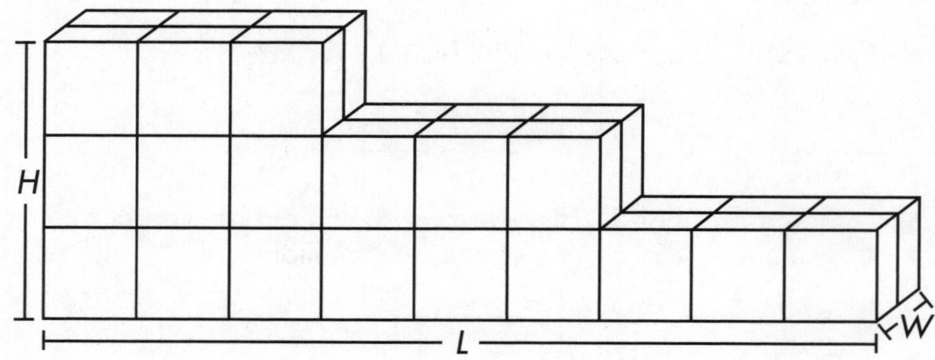

1. Each block in the model is 1 cubic unit. What are the dimensions of the model?

$H =$ __________ $L =$ __________ $W =$ __________

2. If each edge of the unit cubes in the model represents an actual length of 10 ft., what will the dimensions of the actual building be? How did you get these answers?

$H =$ __________ $L =$ __________ $W =$ __________

0-7424-2885-0 *Using the Standards—Algebra*

Name ______________________ Date ____________

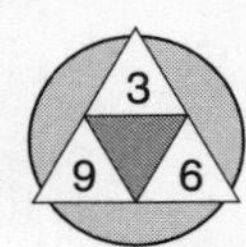

Building Basics (cont.)

3. The builders are trying to decide how big they want the building to be. Complete the following table showing the dimensions of the actual building when the edge of each cube represents different lengths.

each unit (ft.)	10	12	14	16	18	20
H						
L						
W						

4. If *U* stands for the actual length that each edge of the cube represents, write an equation showing how to find each dimension on the actual building.

$H =$ __________ $L =$ __________ $W =$ __________

5. The builders decide to let each edge of a cube represent 12 ft. They need to know how much siding they will need for the building.

a. What type of measurement is this? ______________________

b. How many square units on the model will require siding? ______________

c. How much actual siding will the builders need for each square on the model? Tell how you found this answer.

d. How much actual siding will the builders need for the whole building? Write an equation showing how you found your answer.

DO MORE

How could you find out how many square feet of floor space will be in the actual building? Each layer of cubes in the model represents 1 story.

Name ____________________ Date __________

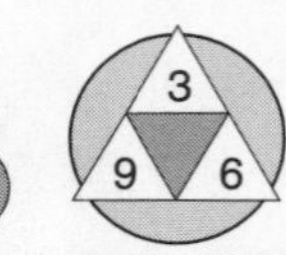

Slippery When Wet

Materials: bucket, water, golf balls, ruler

You may have noticed that the water level in your bathtub rises when you get in. This is called displacement. This also happens in a swimming pool. One person may not displace very much water. But what about 10 people? Or 20? How high should the water level be so the water does not run over the edges of the pool? The following experiment will help you learn more about the concept of displacement.

1. Fill a bucket about $\frac{1}{4}$ full of water. Measure the water level using a ruler.

starting water level = __________

2. Put a golf ball in the water and measure the water level again. Then put two golf balls in the water. Continue adding golf balls and taking water level measurements. Record your answers in the following table.

# golf balls	water level
0	
1	
2	
3	
4	
5	
6	
7	
8	
9	
10	

3. Describe any patterns you see between the number of golf balls and the water level.

Name ______________________ Date __________

Slippery When Wet (cont.)

4. Make a coordinate graph that shows the data in your table.

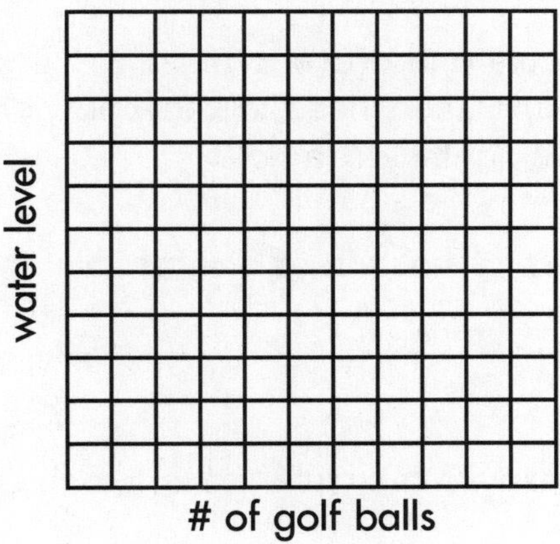

5. Describe the pattern you see in the graph.

6. Let G represent the number of golf balls and W represent the water level. Write an equation showing the relationship between them. ______________________

7. Predict the water level if there were 20 golf balls in the bucket. Explain how you made your prediction.

8. Test your prediction from problem 7. Were you correct?

THINK

Would you have gotten a different pattern if there had been more or less water in the bucket to start with? Would you have gotten a different pattern if the bucket was wider?

 Name ______________________ Date ____________

Column Creations

Materials: $8\frac{1}{2}$ x 11" paper, tape, a stack of books, ruler, scissors

Columns are often used in architecture to add beauty and grace to buildings. But they also have an important role in the structure of the building. Engineers need to know how changes in the dimensions of the columns affect the amount of weight they can hold.

1. What do you think will hold more weight, a tall column or a short column? Why?

2. Follow these instructions to create 5 columns with a circular base. Each column will have the same diameter, but a different height.

Use a piece of $8\frac{1}{2}$ x 11" paper to make each column.

Hold the paper lengthwise and roll it into a cylinder. Tape the edges together so that the sides overlap by $\frac{1}{2}$ inch. You now have a column that is 11 inches tall. The circular base should have a diameter of about $2\frac{1}{2}$ inches.

Cut 1 inch off the length of the paper and then roll it into a cylinder. Tape the edges together so that the sides overlap by $\frac{1}{2}$ inch. The base of this column should have the same diameter as the previous column, but it is only 10 inches tall.

Create 3 more columns with heights of 9, 8, and 7 inches. The diameter of each column should be approximately $2\frac{1}{2}$ inches.

3. Test to see how much weight each column will hold. Place the column on a hard floor. Choose a set of small paperback books that are all about the same size. Carefully place the books on top of the column one by one. Count the number of books the column will hold. Record your results in the table below.

height (in.)	7	8	9	10	11
books					

Name ______________________ Date __________

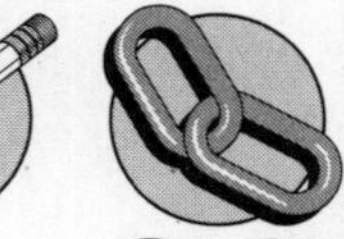

Column Creations (cont.)

4. Make a coordinate graph of the data you collected in problem 3.

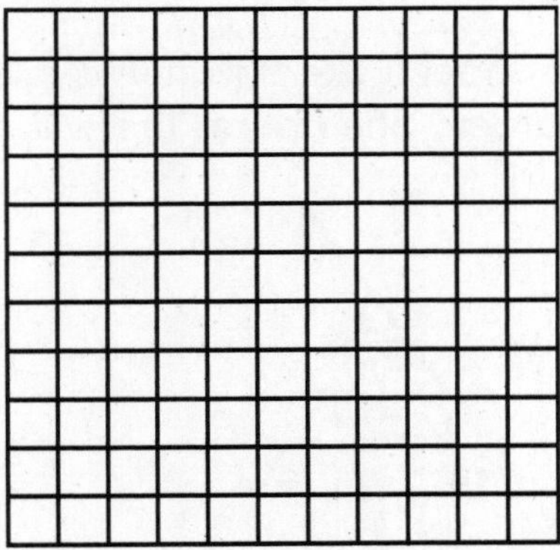

5. Describe any patterns you see in the table and graph.

6. How many books do you think a column that is 12 inches high would hold? How about a column 6 inches high? Explain how you made your prediction.

THINK

What other factors might affect the amount of weight a column can hold?

0-7424-2885-0 *Using the Standards—Algebra*

Name ______________________ Date ____________

How Does Your Garden Grow?

Materials: graph paper

Last year, Ms. Wilder had a vegetable garden shaped like a right triangle. This year she plans to double the length of the fencing around her garden. She figures this will double the amount of area she has for vegetables.

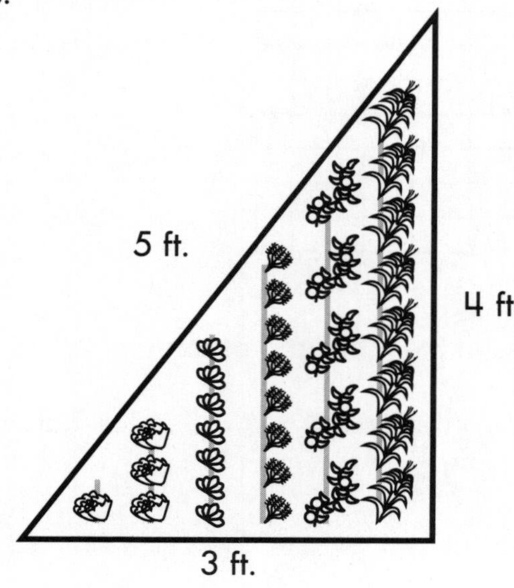

1. Do you agree with Ms. Wilder's reasoning? Will doubling the perimeter cause the area to double also? Explain your reasoning.

2. Use graph paper to draw a model of Ms. Wilder's garden. Draw a right triangle with side lengths of 3, 4, and 5 units. Estimate the area of her garden by counting the number of squares inside the triangle. $A =$ __________

3. Now draw a model of the garden Ms. Wilder wants to make this year. How long will each of the sides of this triangle be?

 Name ________________________ Date ____________

How Does Your Garden Grow? (cont.)

4. Estimate the area of her new garden by counting the number of squares inside the triangle.

   N = __________

5. Compare your answers from problems 2 and 4. How much larger is the area of the new garden?

6. Was Ms. Wilder's reasoning correct? Explain.

7. Mr. Green has a rectangular garden that is 3 ft. by 5 ft. What will happen to the area of his garden if he doubles the perimeter? Use graph paper to model the problem and test your answer.

8. Make a hypothesis about what happens to the area of any shape when its perimeter is doubled. Write an equation that shows this relationship.

DO MORE

How could prove that your hypothesis is true?

Name ______________________ Date __________

Create Your Own Problems

1. Use unit cubes to build a model of a building. Choose a scale for your building. Write some questions about the size of your building and have a friend answer them.

2. Design an experiment involving columns. Change one thing about the columns (shape, diameter, etc.) and see how this affects the amount of weight the column will hold. Make a table and a graph. See if there are any patterns.

3. Make up some questions involving the relationship between perimeter and area of triangles or rectangles. Figure out how to find the answers to your questions by using models.

Name ____________________ Date __________

Check Your Skills

The Medieval Medley Company gives its customers a medieval dining experience, complete with King, a fair princess, jesters, and dashing knights. The show is so successful that they will be moving to a new building. Architects have designed the building to look similar to a castle. A sketch of the building is shown below.

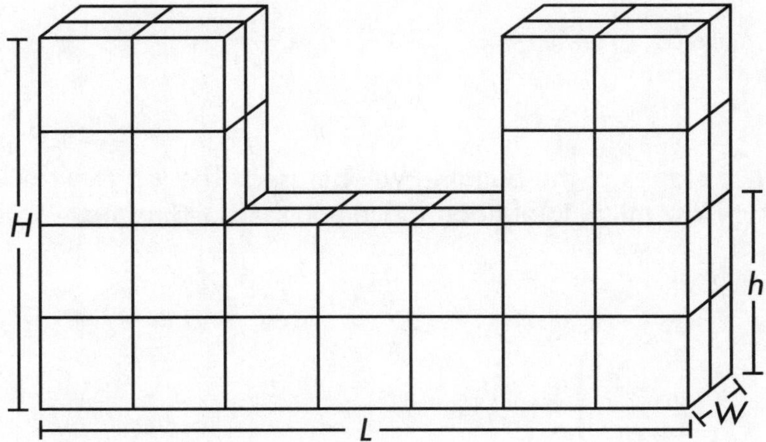

Use unit cubes to make a model of the building shown above. Use the model to help you answer the questions below.

1. An edge of each cube represents U ft. on the actual building. Write equations showing how to find the dimensions of the actual building.

$H =$ ________ $h =$ ________ $L =$ ________ $W =$ ________

2. The builders have decided that $U = 15$ ft. Find the actual dimensions of the building.

$H =$ ________ $h =$ ________ $L =$ ________ $W =$ ________

Name ______________________ Date ____________

Check Your Skills (cont.)

3. What is the volume of the building? Explain how you found your answer.

4. Only the bottom two stories of the building will be used. The top two stories of both towers are only for show. How much total floor space will the building have? Show how you got your answer.

5. The Medieval Medley Company thinks they may need even more space for the jousting events. They decide to double the length and width of the building. How will this affect the amount of floor space available? Explain how you know.

Name ______________________ Date ____________

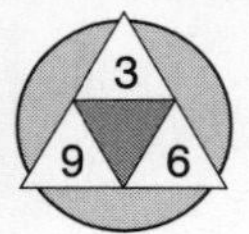

Go the Distance

The following equation can help you find the distance, *D*, an object travels if it moves at a constant rate, *R*, for a period of time, *T*.

$$D = R \times T$$

1. Kayla has 90 minutes to ride her bike before she has to be home for supper. Write an equation showing the relationship between the speed she travels and the amount of distance she can cover during that time. ______________________

2. It is a clear day with little wind, so Kayla figures she can average at least 0.35 kilometers per minute. If she wants to be in time for supper, how far should she go before she turns around to come home? Explain.

3. Kayla can usually average between 0.25 and 0.4 kilometers per minute. Complete the following table showing the total distance she can travel round trip for each average speed.

R	0.25	0.275	0.3	0.325	0.35	0.375	0.4
D							

4. Describe what happens to the distance Kayla can travel when her average speed increases.

DO MORE

There are approximately 1.6 kilometers in every mile. Write an equation showing how to change each distance value in the table from kilometers to miles.

0-7424-2885-0 *Using the Standards—Algebra*

Name ______________________ Date __________

Do You Have the Time?

The following equation can help you find the distance, *D*, an object travels if it moves at a constant rate, *R*, for a period of time, *T*.

$$D = R \times T$$

1. Jordan and his dad are going to take a road trip. They get on the highway where the speed limit is 70 miles per hour. Write an equation showing the relationship between the time they travel on the highway and the distance they cover. ______________

2. They travel 95 miles before reaching their exit. How long did it take them to get to the exit? Explain.

3. Complete the following table showing the time it will take them to travel each distance. Record Time to the nearest $\frac{1}{100}$ of an hour.

T									
D	70	75	80	85	90	95	100	105	110

4. Describe the relationship between distance and time.

DO MORE

There are approximately 1.6 kilometers in every mile. Write an equation showing how to change the distance values in the table from miles to kilometers.

Name ______________________ Date ____________

Speed Zone

The following equation can help you find the distance, *D*, an object travels if it moves at a constant rate, *R*, for a period of time, *T*.

$$D = R \times T$$

1. Maria and her dad are testing out the motorcycle they rebuilt. They ride to a nearby town. The town is 100 miles away. Write an equation showing the relationship between the time of the trip and their average speed. ______________________

2. It took them 2.5 hours to get to the town traveling on a two-lane highway. What was their average speed? Explain.

3. Complete the following table showing the average speed they need to travel to make the trip in the given amount of time. Round the speed values to the nearest mile per hour.

T	1.5	2	2.5	3	3.5
R					

4. Describe the relationship between rate and time.

THINK

Explain how to find time values if you know rates.

Name ______________________ Date ____________

Coaster Chronicles

The Rocket roller coaster ride is the main attraction at the Wonder Planet Amusement Park. The following graph shows the riders' height from the ground at each second of the ride. Use the graph to answer the questions.

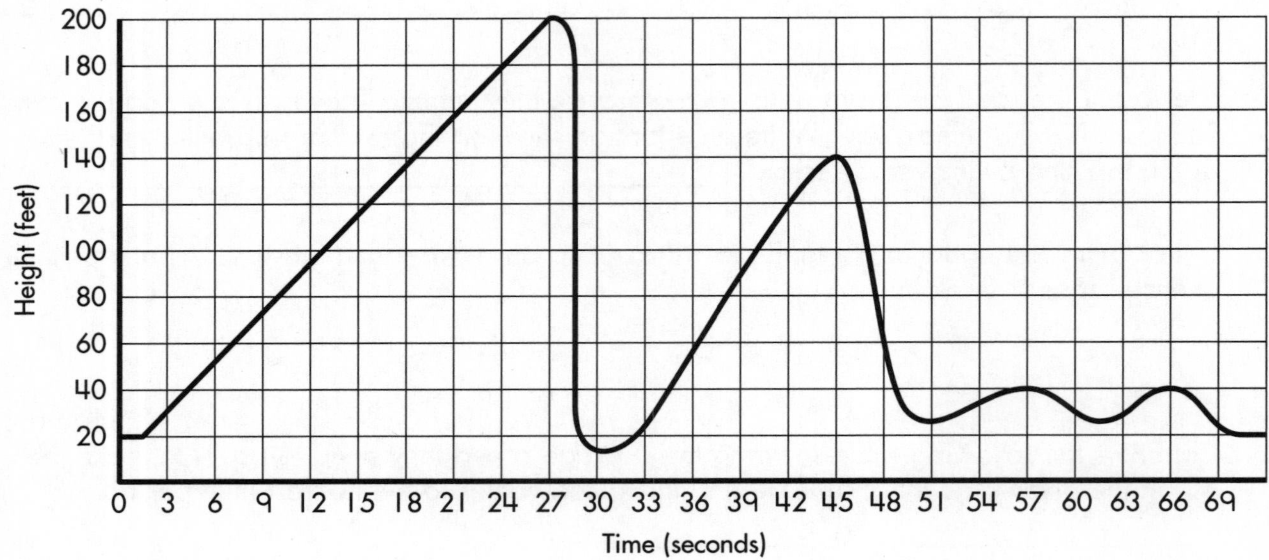

1. How does the height change for the first 27 seconds of the ride? What is happening at this time?

2. How long does the ride last? ______________________________

3. Do the riders spend more time going uphill or downhill? Tell how you arrived at your answer.

Name ______________________ Date ____________

Coaster Chronicles (cont.)

4. At what time do the riders reach the lowest point? How far from the ground are they?

5. At what time do the riders reach the highest point? How far from the ground are they?

6. Do you think the Rocket is actually shaped like the graph? Why or why not?

7. Over what time interval is the roller coaster traveling the fastest? What is happening on the ride at that time?

8. Describe what is happening on the roller coaster throughout the ride. Be sure to include specific times in your description.

THINK

Do you think this would be a fun roller coaster to ride? Why or why not?

Name ______________________ Date __________

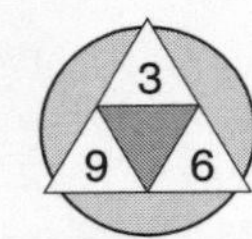

What's the Cost?

A group of students and chaperones are going on a trip to the theatre. The school got a special deal, where the total cost of the trip is $300 for any number of people up to 75.

1. If 40 people went on the trip and split the costs evenly, how much did each person pay? Show how you arrived at your answer.

2. Let P represent the number of people going on the trip. Let C represent the cost per person. Write an equation showing how to find the cost per person if you know the number of people going on the trip.

   $C =$ ____

3. Complete the following table showing the cost per person, depending on how many people go on the trip. Record your answers to the nearest penny.

P	C
5	
10	
15	
20	
25	
30	
35	
40	
45	
50	
55	
60	
65	
70	
75	

Name ____________________ Date ____________

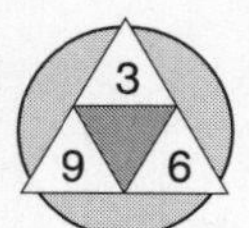

What's the Cost? (cont.)

4. Describe what happens to the cost per person as the number of people increases.

5. What do you think the graph of this data will look like? Will it increase or decrease from left to right? What kind of shape will it have?

6. Check your answer to problem 4 by making a coordinate graph of the data.

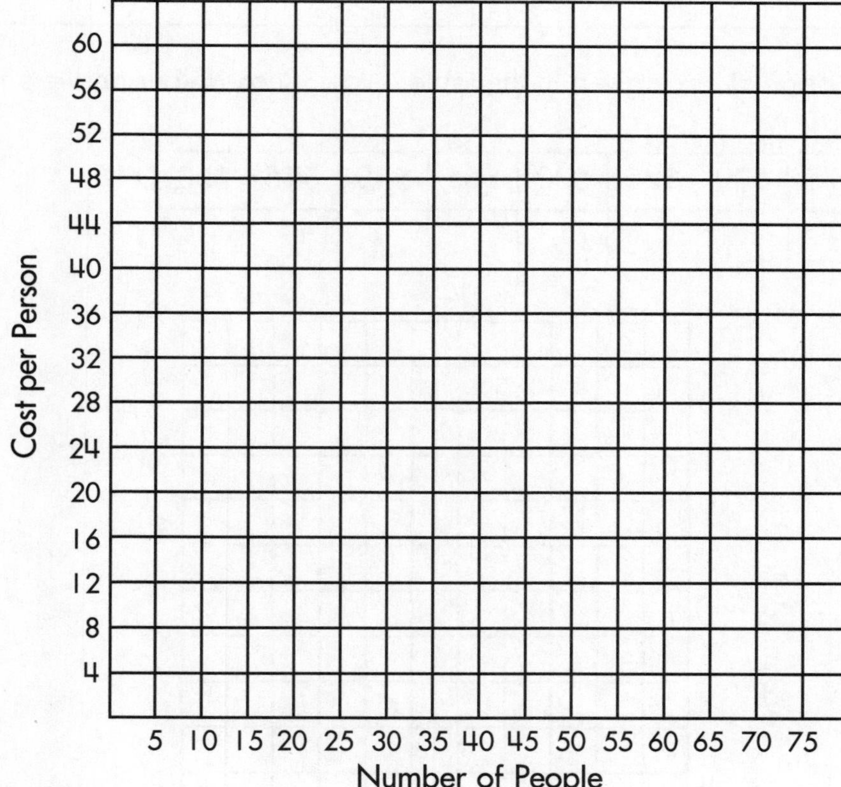

THINK

Does the graph look the way you expected it would? Why do you think the graph has the shape that it does?

Name ______________________ Date ____________

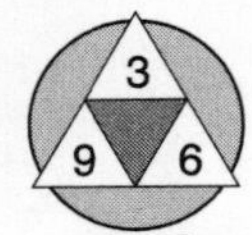

Discount Extravaganza

Superior Sports is having a huge sale. Every piece of sports equipment is 25% off.

1. Laura wants a pair of ice skates that normally cost $45. How much will she save on the skates? Show your work.

2. Let P represent the original price of a piece of sports equipment. Let D represent the amount of the discount. Write an equation showing how to find the discount based on the original price of the item.

D = ____

3. Find the discount for each original price given in the table below. Record your answers to the nearest penny.

P	$5	$10	$15	$20	$25	$30	$35	$40	$45	$50
D										

4. Make a coordinate graph of the data from problem 2.

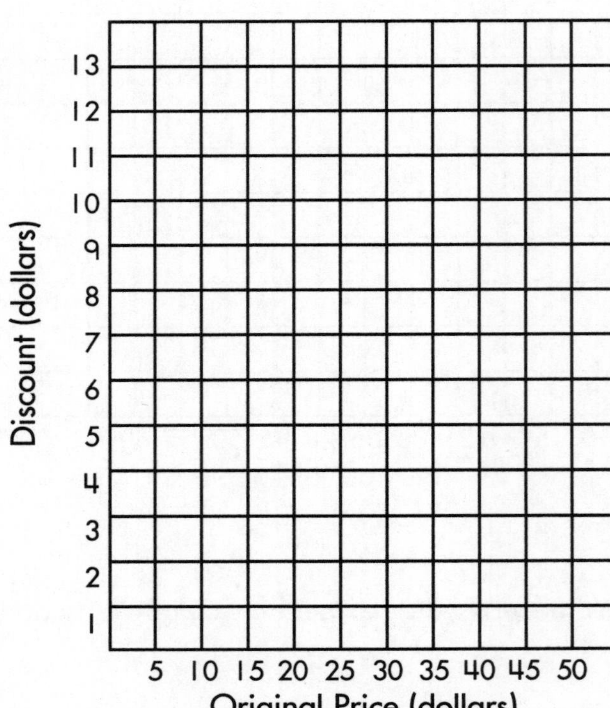

Name ______________________ Date __________

Discount Extravaganza (cont.)

5. Describe the relationship between the original price and the amount of the discount.

6. How much will Laura's ice skates cost after the discount? Show your work.

7. Let P represent the original price of a piece of sports equipment. Let S represent the sale price. Write an equation showing how to find the sale price based on the original price of the item.

$S =$ ____

8. Find the sale price for each original price given in the table below. Record your answers to the nearest penny.

P	\$5	\$10	\$15	\$20	\$25	\$30	\$35	\$40	\$45	\$50
D										

9. Make a coordinate graph of the data from problem 8 on a separate piece of graph paper.

10. Describe what happens to the sale price as the original price of an item increases.

THINK

Compare the graphs and tables of the discount and sale price. How are they similar? How are they different?

Name ____________________ Date __________

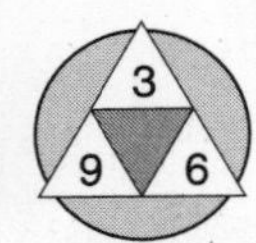

A Bit of Bounce

If the difference between each pair of numbers is the same, then the function has a **constant rate of change**.

If the difference between each pair of numbers gets larger, then the function has an **increasing rate of change**.

If the difference between each pair of numbers gets smaller, then the function has a **decreasing rate of change**.

A particular rubber ball dropped from a height of 16 ft. will rebound to $\frac{3}{4}$ of its previous height on each bounce.

1. Make a table showing the height of the ball after each bounce. Record the height to the nearest tenth of a foot.

# bounces	0	1	2	3	4	5	6
height (ft.)	16	12					

2. Make a coordinate graph of the data. Be sure to label your axes and include a scale.

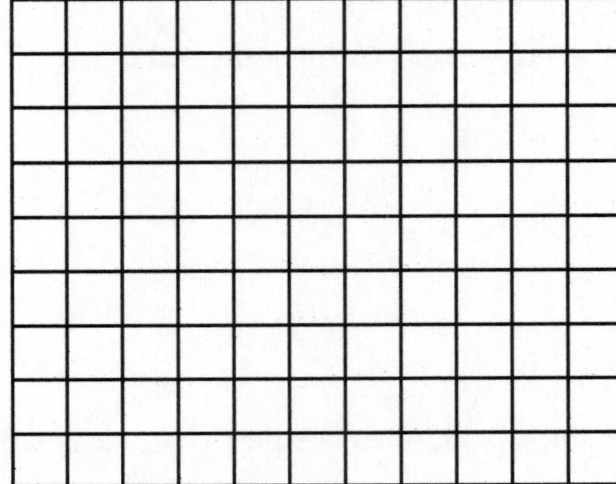

0-7424-2885-0 *Using the Standards—Algebra*

Name ______________________ Date ____________

A Bit of Bounce (cont.)

3. Find the amount of change in the height from one value to the next. Does the height decrease at a constant, increasing, or decreasing rate?

4. Look at the graph. How is the type of change (constant, increasing, or decreasing) shown by the shape of the graph?

5. A different ball dropped from a height of 16 ft. will rebound to half its height on each bounce. Make a table showing the height of the ball at each bounce.

# bounces	0	1	2	3	4	5	6
height (ft.)	16	8					

6. Make a graph of this data on a separate piece of graph paper. Does the height of this ball decrease at a constant, increasing, or decreasing rate? How do you know?

DO MORE

Compare the graphs and tables showing the heights of the two different balls. What is similar? What is different?

Name ______________________ Date ____________

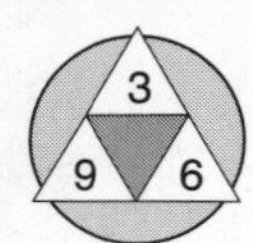

Aquarium Arrangements

If the difference between each pair of numbers in the pattern is the same, then the function has a **constant rate of change**.

If the difference between each pair of numbers gets larger, then the function has an **increasing rate of change**.

If the difference between each pair of numbers gets smaller, then the function has a **decreasing rate of change**.

Alisha's father is building a custom aquarium into a wall of their house. The tank will be 19 inches wide and 74 inches long. Alisha's father is trying to decide how tall he wants the tank to be.

1. Write an equation showing how to find the volume *V*, of the tank for a given height *H*.

   V = ____

2. Find the volume of the tank for each possible height given in the table.

H (in.)	24	25	26	27	28	29	30
V (in.^{3})							

3. What happens to the volume as the height increases by 1 inch?

4. Does the volume change at a constant rate, an increasing rate, or a decreasing rate? How do you know?

0-7424-2885-0 *Using the Standards—Algebra*

Name ____________________ Date __________

Aquarium Arrangements (cont.)

5. Make a coordinate graph of the data in problem 2.

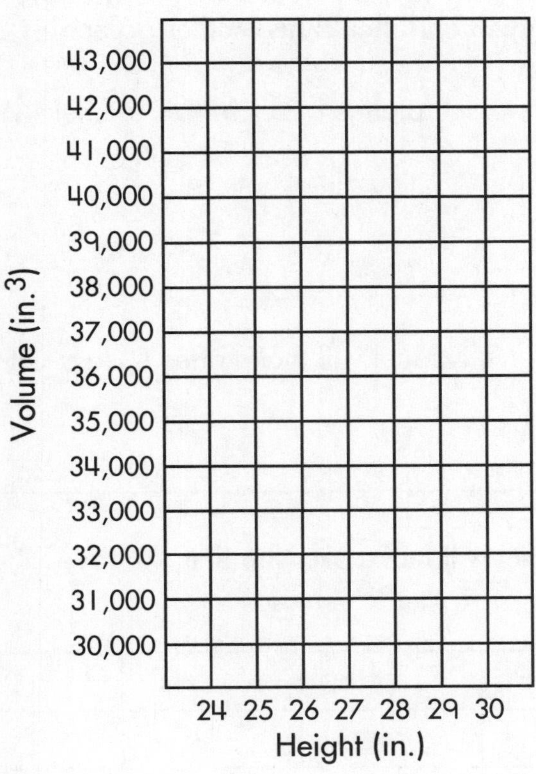

6. How does the shape of the graph relate to the volume's rate of change?

DO MORE

Alisha's father wants about a 150-gallon tank. There are 231 cubic inches in a gallon. How many cubic inches would be needed for a 150-gallon tank? Which height should Alisha's father make the aquarium? Show your work.

0-7424-2885-0 *Using the Standards—Algebra*

Name ______________________ Date __________

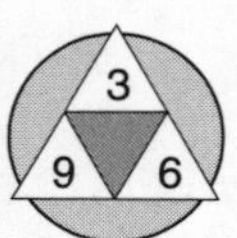

Payment Plans

Miguel's mother offers to pay him to do some extra chores around the house. She says she'll pay him $3 a day. Miguel says he wants only 1 penny the first day, 2 pennies the second day, 4 pennies the third day, 8 pennies the fourth day, and so on. Should his mother accept his offer?

1. Which plan do you think is better for Miguel? Which plan is better for his mother? Why?

2. Write an equation showing how much money, M, Miguel will make after D days with his mother's plan.

M = ______________________________

3. Make a table showing how much money Miguel will make over the first 10 days if he takes his mother's offer.

D	1	2	3	4	5	6	7	8	9	10	11	12
M	3											

4. Is there a constant or varying rate of change in the total earned under his mother's plan? Explain.

5. Make a table showing how much money Miguel will make each day if his mother accepts his offer. Then calculate the total amount he would have made up to that point.

# of days	1	2	3	4	5	6	7	8	9	10	11	12
amt. earned	0.01	0.02	0.04	0.08								
total earned	0.01	0.03	0.07	0.15								

0-7424-2885-0 *Using the Standards—Algebra*

Name ______________________ Date ____________

Payment Plans (cont.)

6. Is there a constant or varying rate of change in the total earned under Miguel's mother's plan? Explain.

7. Compare the tables. Which plan would be better for Miguel if he only worked 10 days? Explain.

8. If Miguel works 15 days, which plan would be better for him? Explain.

9. Under what conditions would it be best for Miguel to accept his mother's offer? Explain.

10. Under what conditions would it be best for Miguel to use his own plan? Explain.

THINK

Did the results of the two plans turn out the way you thought they would?

Name ____________________ Date __________

What Goes Up Must Come Down

If a function has a **constant rate of change**, then the difference between each pair of numbers in the pattern is the same.

If the difference between each pair of numbers gets larger, then the function has an **increasing rate of change**.

If the difference between each pair of numbers gets smaller, then the function has a **decreasing rate of change**.

A baseball is hit into the air. The following graph shows the height of the ball above the ground at any particular time. Use the graph to answer the following questions.

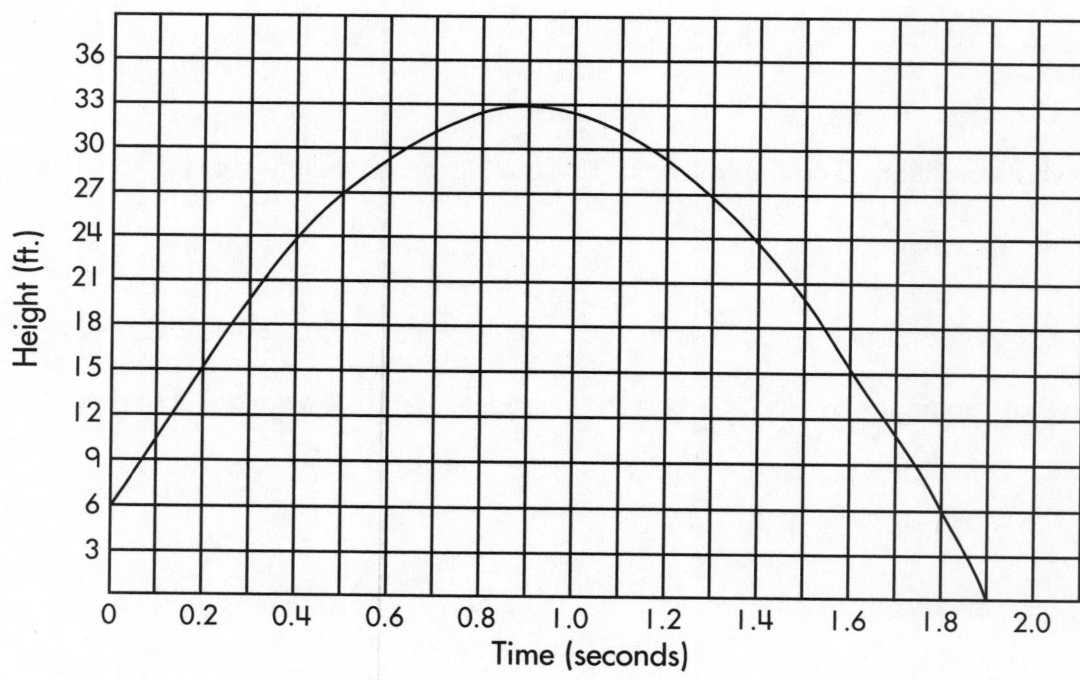

1. How high was the ball off the ground when it was hit? ____________________

0-7424-2885-0 *Using the Standards—Algebra*

Name ______________________ Date ____________

What Goes Up Must Come Down (cont.)

2. When did the ball reach its maximum height, and how high was it from the ground?

____

3. When did the ball hit the ground? ______________________________

4. Use the graph to estimate the height of the ball at the times given in the table.

T	0.1	0.3	0.5	0.7	0.9	1.1	1.3	1.5	1.7	1.9
H										

5. Over what time intervals did the height of the ball increase? ________________

6. As the height increased, did it change at a constant, increasing, or decreasing rate? How do you know?

7. Over what time intervals did the height of the ball decrease? ________________

8. As the height decreased, did it change at a constant, increasing, or decreasing rate? How do you know?

THINK

How can you identify the type of rate of change in the height by looking at the shape of the graph?

Name ______________________ Date ____________

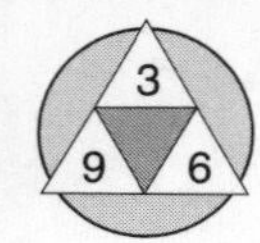

Phone Tree

If the difference between each pair of numbers in the pattern is the same, then the function has a **constant rate of change**.

If the difference between each pair of numbers gets larger, then the function has an **increasing rate of change**.

If the difference between each pair of numbers gets smaller, then the function has a **decreasing rate of change**.

The Southtown Soccer Club uses a phone tree to make sure everyone gets notified in case of rain cancellations. The President of the club calls two members. Each of these two people call two more.

1. Complete the diagram below to show how many people get called at the first 4 stages.

stage 0

stage 1

stage 2

stage 3

stage 4

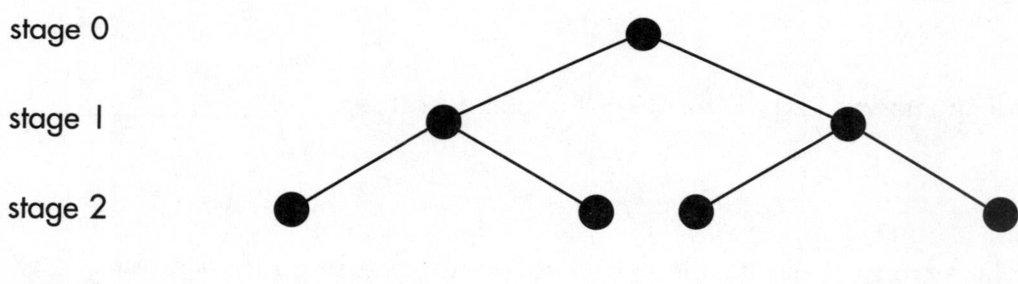

2. Complete the following table showing how many phone calls are made at each stage. Use the diagram to help you. Then find a pattern to help you complete the table.

stage	0	1	2	3	4	5	6	7
# calls	1	2	4					

Name ______________________ Date ____________

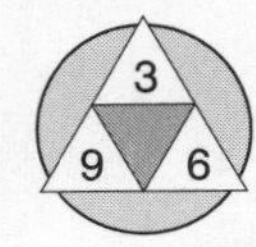

Phone Tree (cont.)

3. Graph the number of calls made at each of the first seven stages.

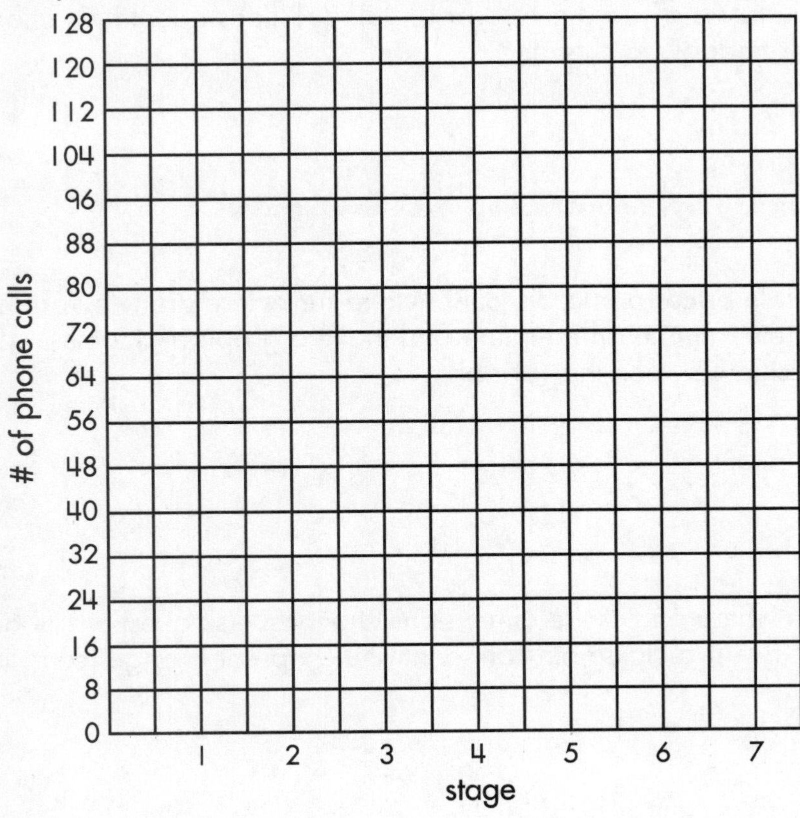

4. Do the number of calls increase at a constant, increasing, or decreasing rate? How do you know?

5. How does the shape of the graph show the type of change you identified in problem 4?

DO MORE

If the phone tree goes to four stages, how many total people will have been called?

Name ______________________ Date ____________

Create Your Own Problems

1. Write a problem that relates distance, speed, and time. Ask a classmate to write an equation, make a table, and make a coordinate graph. Ask questions about how changing one variable causes another variable to change.

2. Write a problem involving sale prices and a discount. Make sure there are two variables in your problem. Ask a classmate to write an equation and make a graph and table. Ask questions about the relationship between the variables.

3. Make up a volume problem where one of the dimensions changes. Ask questions about how this affects the volume. See if a classmate can identify the type of change (constant, increasing, or decreasing).

4. Sketch three different graphs, each with a different rate of change. Ask a classmate to decide which graph shows a constant rate of change and which graphs show an increasing or decreasing rate of change.

Name ______________________ Date ____________

Check Your Skills

1. Julia's family is going on a road trip. They average 65 miles per hour the first day.

a. Write an equation showing the relationship between the time, *T*, and the distance, *D*, they traveled. ______________________

b. Complete the table below showing how far they went if they traveled for the given amount of time.

time (hrs.)	1	2	3	4	5	6	7	8
distance (miles)								

c. Describe how the distance changes as the time increases.

d. Does the distance change at a constant, increasing, or decreasing rate? How do you know?

2. The Superintendent of Fairview Schools decides to call a snow day. He starts a phone tree to let all the teachers and administrators know that school is cancelled. He calls 3 people and each of them calls 3 more people.

a. Make a diagram showing 3 stages of the phone tree.

b. Complete the table showing the first 5 stages of the phone tree.

stage	0	1	2	3	4	5
# calls						

c. Make a coordinate graph of the data from problem 2b on a separate piece of graph paper.

d. Do the number of calls increase at a constant, increasing, or decreasing rate? How do you know?

Name ______________________ Date ___________

Check Your Skills (cont.)

3. A particular rubber ball bounces $\frac{2}{3}$ of its height at each consecutive bounce. It started at a height of 72 inches.

a. Complete the table below showing the ball's height for the first 8 bounces. Write the height to the nearest tenth of an inch.

# bounces	0	1	2	3	4	5	6	7	8
height									

b. Make a coordinate graph showing the relationship between the number of bounces and the ball's height above the ground.

c. Does the height of the ball decrease at a constant rate, an increasing rate, or a decreasing rate? Explain.

4. Look at each of the graphs. Each graph increases from left to right, but they have different rates of change. Write constant, increasing, or decreasing to identify the type of rate of change for each graph.

a.

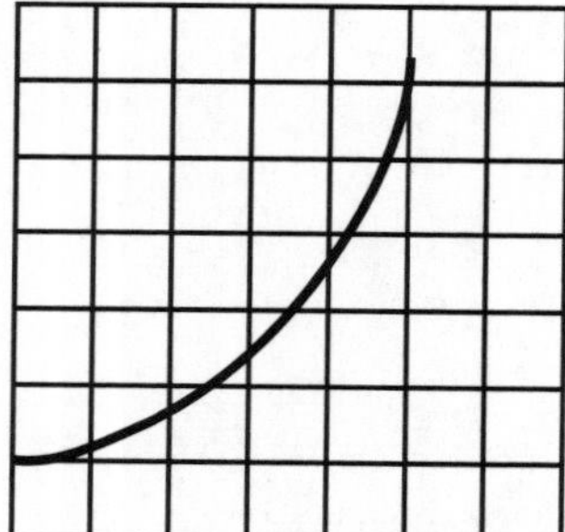

b.

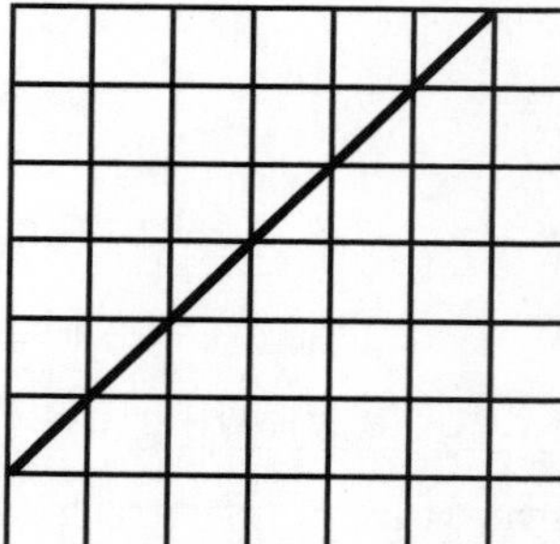

c.

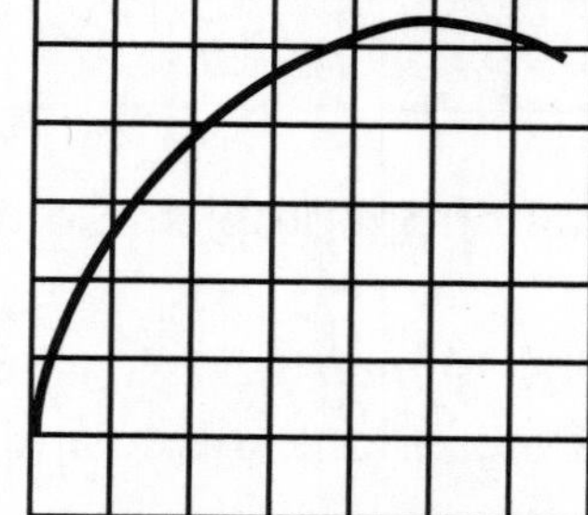

Name ______________________ Date ____________

Posttest

1. Find the next three numbers in each pattern. Describe each of the following patterns. Circle the one(s) that grow at a constant rate.

a. 5, 6, 8, 11, 15, 20, ____, ____, ____ __________

b. 12, 17, 29, 46, 75, 121, ____, ____, ____ __________

c. 6, 9, 12, 15, 18, 21, ____, ____, ____ __________

2. A function machine uses a rule to change numbers. Look for a pattern between the IN and OUT numbers in the table. Fill in the missing numbers. Write the rule.

IN	10	6		22	18	44
OUT	22		27	34		56

Rule: ______________________________

3. Each symbol stands for a number. Find the numbers that make both equations true.

a.  = 42

 ÷ = 8

 = __________

 = __________

b. ♡ x ◇ = 300

♡ ÷ ◇ = 12

♡ = __________

◇ = __________

4. Alita owes her brother $100. She is paying back $5 a week.

a. Let *O* be the amount Alita owes and *W* be the number of weeks she has been paying her brother. Write an equation showing the relationship between *O* and *W*.

b. If Alita has been paying her brother for 9 weeks, how much does she still owe?

c. If Alita owes her brother $40, how many weeks has she been paying him back?

d. Describe the relationship between the number of weeks and the amount Alita owes.

Name ______________________ Date __________

Posttest (cont.)

5. Look at the pattern in the tiles shown. Use squares or tiles to make the patterns.

stage 0

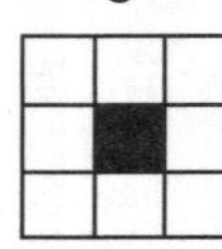

stage 1

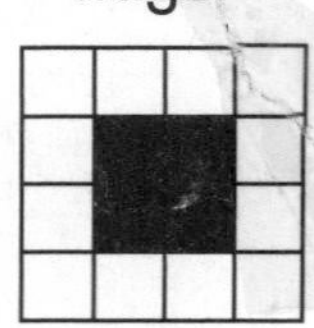

stage 2

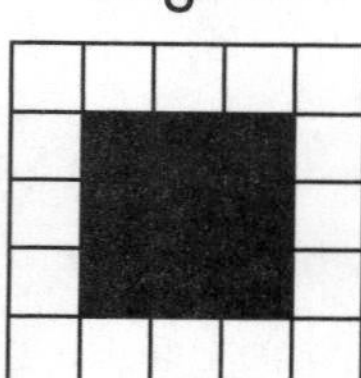

a. Build the next two models in the pattern.

b. Make a table showing the relationship between the stage and the number of white squares.

stage	0	1	2	3	4	5
# white						

c. Does the number of white squares increase at a constant, increasing, or decreasing rate? How do you know?

d. Make a table showing the relationship between the stage and the number of black squares.

stage	0	1	2	3	4	5
# black						

e. Does the number of black squares increase at a constant, increasing, or decreasing rate? How do you know?

f. Which of the following graphs most likely shows the number of white squares? Which shows the number of black squares?

I.

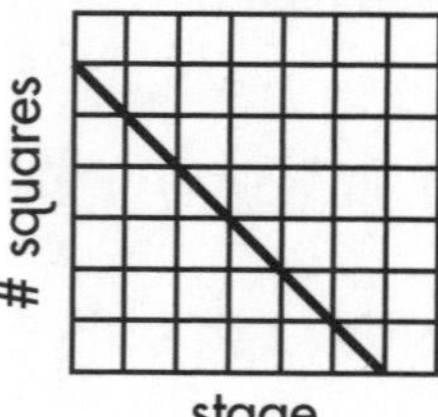

II.

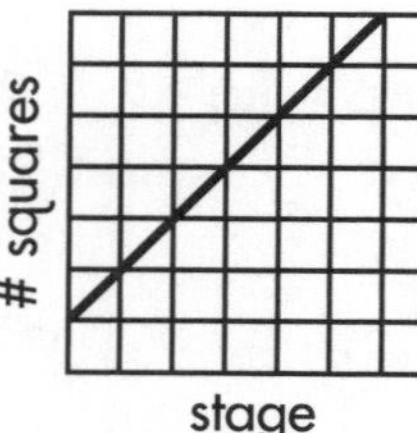

III.

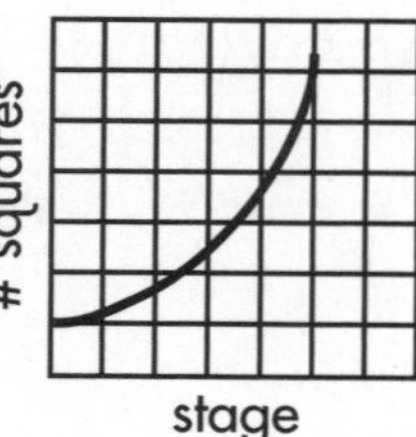

IV.

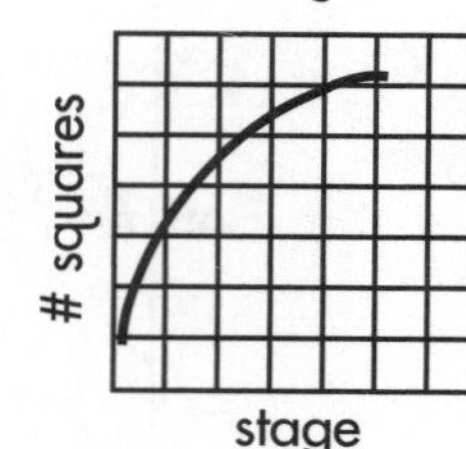

Answer Key

Pretest . . . . **pages 7–8**

1. a. 512, 323, 134; –189; decreasing
b. 1,536; 6,144; 24,576; x 4; increasing
c. 25, 81, 81; ABB; repeating

2.

IN	84	90	54	36	72	30
OUT	14	15	9	6	12	5

Rule: OUT = IN ÷ 6

3. a. associative
b. commutative
c. distributive

4. a. $V = 214$
b. $T = 1{,}566$
c. $W = 92$
d. $S = 242$

5. $C = 30$, $L = 15$, $P = 6$, $S = 9$

6. a. $R = 600 \div T$
b.

T	7	8	9	10	11	12	13	14	15
R	85.7	75	66.7	60	54.5	50	46.2	42.9	40

c. The speed decreases as the time increases.
d. The speed decreases at a decreasing rate. The difference between speed values gets smaller each time.

7. a. Perimeter = 52 ft. Area = 168 sq. ft.
b. The perimeter will double. $N = 2 \times P$
c. The area will be 4 times larger. $M = A \times 4$

8. a. $D = 0.30 \times R$
b. Graph B

Move to the Rhythm . . . . **page 9**

1. Check students' dance rhythms to make sure they match the letter patterns.
2. The pattern is the same, even when different movements are assigned to the letter. But, the dance will look much different.

Jumpin' Jigsaws . . . . **page 10**

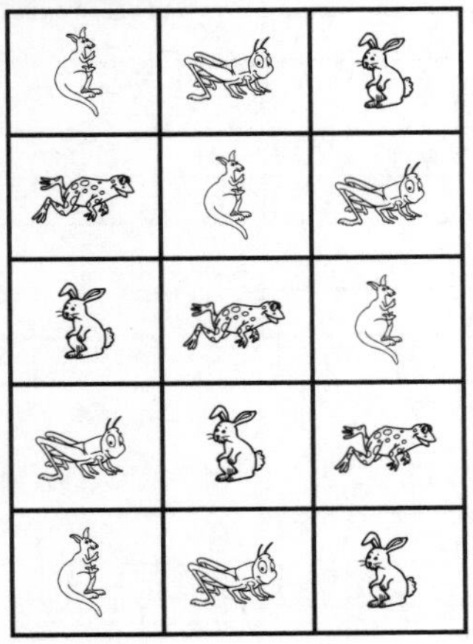

Shape Up . . . . **page 11**

1. 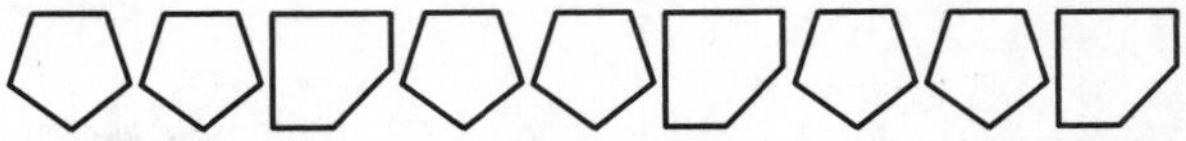
2. 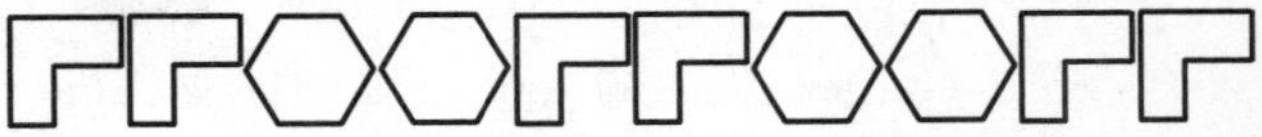
3. 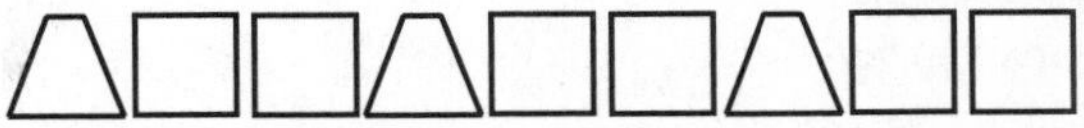
4.

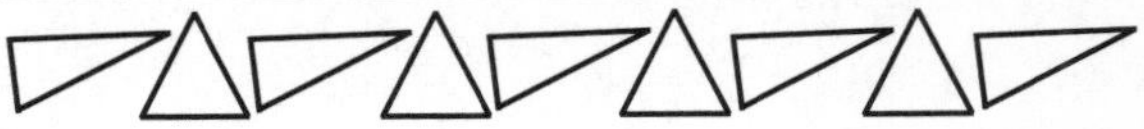

Nutty Numerals . . . . **page 12**

1. 23, 23, 14, 23, 23, 14, 23, 23, 14; AAB
2. 45, 37, 11, 45, 37, 11, 45, 37, 11; ABC
3. 66, 66, 84, 84 66, 66, 84, 84, 66, 66; AABB
4. 92, 54, 54, 87, 92, 54, 54, 87, 92, 54; ABBC
5. 28, 28, 48, 28, 28, 48, 28, 28, 48; AAB
6. 105, 99, 354, 105, 99, 354, 105, 99, 354; ABC

It's a Match . . . . **page 13**

1. E, II
2. A, V
3. C, I
4. B, III
5. D, IV

Growing and Shrinking . . . . **page 14**

1. 590 662 734; growing; + 72
2. 6,066 5,438 4,810; decreasing; – 628
3. 1,369 929, 489; decreasing; – 440
4. 1,044 1,099 1,154; increasing; + 55

Climbing and Falling . . . . **page 15**

1. 11,250; 56,250; 281,250; growing; x 5
2. 450; 90; 18; decreasing; ÷ 5
3. 448; 56; 7; decreasing; ÷ 8
4. 28,672; 229,376; 1,835,008; x 8

By the Rules . . . . **page 16**

1. 3 12 48 192 768 3,072 12,288 49,152; x 4
2. 350,000,000 35,000,000 3,500,000 350,000 35,000 3,500 350 35; ÷ 10
3. 8,275 7,942 7,609 7,276 6,943 6,610 6,277 5,944; – 333
4. 340 526 712 898 1,084 1,270 1,456 1,642; + 186

A Rule in Time . . . . **page 17**

1. 55 94 133 172 211 250 289 328; + 39
2. 15,309 5,103 1,701 567 189 63 21 7; ÷ 3
3. 905 831 757 683 609 535 461 387; – 74
4. 5 20 80 320 1,280 5,120 20,480 81,920; x 4

Answer Key

Building Blocks .pages 18–19

1. 3, 6, 9
2. + 3
3. 12, 15, 18
4. Build the next 3 models and count the blocks to find the volume.
5. 14, 22, 30
6. + 8
7. 38, 46, 54
8. Build the next 3 models and count the number of square units on the surface of the model.

Changing Constantly . . . . .pages 20–21

1. Rule: + 31
   - **a.** 31; 31; 31; 31
   - **b.** Yes. The difference between each pair of numbers is 31.
2. Rule: x 3
   - **a.** 324; 108; 36; 12
   - **b.** No. The difference between each pair of numbers is different.
3. Rule: x 6
   - **a.** 4,320; 720; 120; 20
   - **b.** No. The difference between each pair of numbers is different.
4. Rule: + 22
   - **a.** 22; 22; 22; 22
   - **b.** Yes. The difference between each pair of numbers is 22.

Steady Does It . . . . .pages 22–23

1. Rule: – 56
   - **a.** 56; 56; 56; 56
   - **b.** Yes. The difference between each pair of numbers is 56.
2. Rule: ÷ 4
   - **a.** 576; 144; 36; 9
   - **b.** No. The difference between each pair of numbers is different.
3. Rule: – 69
   - **a.** 69; 69; 69; 69
   - **b.** Yes. The difference between each pair of numbers is 69.
4. Rule: ÷ 2
   - **a.** 56; 28; 14; 7
   - **b.** No. The difference between each pair of numbers is different.

Patterns of Change . . . . .pages 24–25

1. 27, 33, 40; Starting with 1, add the next consecutive integer each time (+ 1, + 2, + 3, + 4, + 5, + 6, + 7).
2. 58, 94, 152; To get the next number in the pattern, add the previous two numbers.
3. 48, 43, 39; Starting with 10, subtract the next smallest whole number each time. (– 10, – 9, – 8, – 7, – 6, – 5, – 4).
4. 69, 65, 63; Starting with 14, subtract the next smallest even integer each time. (– 14, –12, – 10, – 8, – 6, – 4, – 2).
5. 211, 340, 551; To get the next number in the pattern, add the previous two numbers.
6. 38, 49, 62; Starting with 1, add the next consecutive odd integer each time. (+ 1, + 3, + 5, + 7, + 9, + 11, + 13).
7. 235, 225, 217; Starting with 20, subtract the next smallest even integer. (– 20, – 18, – 16, – 14, – 12, – 10, – 8).
8. 76, 123, 199; To get the next number in the pattern, add the previous two numbers.

Functions Rule! . . . . .page 26

1.

IN	5	19	21	6	13
OUT	15	57	63	18	39

Rule: x 3

2.

IN	2	8	9	14	28
OUT	25	31	32	37	51

Rule: + 23

3.

IN	82	68	142	71	90
OUT	26	12	86	15	34

Rule: – 56

4.

IN	64	100	92	124	16
OUT	16	25	23	31	4

Rule: ÷ 4

The Ins and Outs . . . . .page 27

1.

IN	15	28	70	42	35	14
OUT	6	19	61	33	26	5

Rule: – 9

2.

IN	4	7	8	14	11	6
OUT	28	49	56	98	77	42

Rule: x 7

3.

IN	25	19	22	74	81	33
OUT	7	1	4	56	63	15

Rule: – 18

4.

IN	36	48	84	108	180	96
OUT	3	4	7	9	15	8

Rule: ÷ 12

Rule Reversal . . . . .page 28

1.

IN	27	80	33	8	56
OUT	79	132	85	60	108

2.

IN	31	54	99	85	46
OUT	12	35	80	66	27

Answer Key

3.

IN	3	8	10	5	4
OUT	39	104	130	65	52

4.

IN	30	42	72	48	54
OUT	5	7	12	8	9

Word Power .... .page 29

1.

IN	0	4	16	31
OUT	40	44	56	71

2. IN: # of grapes José eats.
   OUT: # of grapes Miguel eats.
   Rule: OUT = IN – 15

IN	15	20	34	43
OUT	0	5	19	28

3. IN: # of fish Deshawn has
   OUT: # of fish Tarnell has
   Rule: OUT = 3 x IN

IN	13	6	5	18
OUT	39	18	15	54

4. IN: # problems Bobby got correct
   OUT: # problems Keidra got correct
   Rule: OUT = IN + 11

IN	89	87	69	60
OUT	100	98	80	71

It Takes Two .... .page 30

1. Rule 1: OUT = IN + 5; Rule 2: OUT = IN – 8
2. Rule 1: OUT = IN ÷ 5; Rule 2: OUT = IN + 4
3. Rule 1: OUT = IN x 9; Rule 2: OUT = IN – 12

Double Trouble .... .page 31

1.

Carly **(IN)**	3	5	6	8	10
Julie **(OUT)**	6	10	12	16	20

Rule: OUT = IN x 2

Julie **(IN)**	6	10	12	16	20
Andrea **(OUT)**	1	5	7	11	15

Rule: OUT = IN – 5

2.

Carlos **(IN)**	12	24	36	48	60
Gabriel **(OUT)**	24	36	48	60	72

Rule: OUT = IN + 12

Gabriel **(IN)**	24	36	48	60	72
Tashon **(OUT)**	12	18	24	30	36

Rule: OUT = IN ÷ 2

Check Your Skills .... .page 33

1. a. 2,592; 15,552; 93,312; growing; x 6
   b. 51, 39, 27; decreasing; –12
   c. 15, 7, 15; repeating; ABAB
2. a. 34, 46, 60; add the next consecutive even integer each time (+ 2, + 4, + 6 . . .); not constant
   b. 21, 27, 34; add the next consecutive integer each time (+ 1, + 2, + 3...); not constant
   c. 52, 60, 68; add 8 each time; constant

3.

IN	13	25	16	39	22	72
OUT	39	75	48	117	66	216

Rule: OUT = IN x 3

A Matter of Order .... .page 34

1. 1,721 + 589 = 2,310; 589 + 1,721 = 2,310
2. 876 – 245 = 631; 245 – 876 = ⁻631
3. 75 – 43 = 32; 43 – 75 = ⁻32
4. 86 + 325 = 411; 325 + 86 = 411
5. 782 – 543 = 239; 543 – 782 = ⁻239
6. 2,301 + 1,746 = 4,047; 1,746 + 2,301 = 4,047
7. 658 + 702 = 1,360; 702 + 658 = 1,360
8. 67 – 33= 34; 33 – 67 = ⁻34

A Short Commute .... .page 35

1. 56 x 71 = 3,976; 71 x 56 = 3,976
2. 40 ÷ 8 = 5; 8 ÷ 40 = $\frac{1}{5}$
3. 23 x 18 = 414; 18 x 23 = 414
4. 180 ÷ 12 = 15; 12 ÷ 180 = $\frac{1}{15}$
5. 66 ÷ 11 = 6; 11 ÷ 66 = $\frac{1}{6}$
6. 13 x 45 = 585; 45 x 13 = 585
7. 41 x 86 = 3,526; 86 x 41 = 3,526
8. 384 ÷ 16 = 24; 16 ÷ 384 = $\frac{1}{24}$

Awesome Associations .... .page 36

1. 17 + (34 + 25) = 17 + 59 = 76
2. They grouped the numbers differently. They got the same answer.
3. (52 – 36) – 15 = 16 – 15 = 1
4. They grouped the numbers differently. They got different answers.

Great Groups .... .page 37

1. (18 x 4) x 21 = 72 x 21 = 1,512
2. They grouped the numbers differently. They got the same answer.
3. 18 ÷ (2 ÷ 3) = 18 ÷ $\frac{2}{3}$ = 18 x $\frac{3}{2}$ = 27
4. They grouped the numbers differently. They got different answers.

To Commute or Not to Commute .... .page 38

1. 87 + 15
2. NA
3. 56 x 33
4. 88 + 12
5. 27 x 12
6. NA
7. NA
8. 524 + 613
9. NA

With Whom to Associate? .... .page 39

1. NA
2. NA
3. (251 + 88) + 31
4. 4 x (15 x 8)
5. 22 + (76 + 91)
6. (3 x 14) x 5
7. 12 x (7 x 2)
8. (415 + 88) + 21
9. NA

Answer Key

Proper Properties . . . .**page 40**

1. $9 + 1 + 7 + 3 + 6 + 4 + 8$ commutative
   $(9 + 1) + (7 + 3) + (6 + 4) + 8$ associative
   $10 + 10 + 10 + 8 = 38$
2. $8 + 2 + 6 + 4 + 5 + 5 + 3 + 7$ commutative
   $(8 + 2) + (6 + 4) + (5 + 5) + (3 + 7)$ associative
   $10 + 10 + 10 + 10 = 40$
3. $6 + 4 + 3 + 7 + 2 + 6$ commutative
   $(6 + 4) + (3 + 7) + (2 + 6)$ associative
   $10 + 10 + 8 = 28$
4. $1 + 6 + 4 + 3 + 7 + 5 + 5$ commutative
   $1 + (6 + 4) + (3 + 7) + (5 + 5)$ associative
   $1 + 10 + 10 + 10 = 31$
5. $1 + 9 + 3 + 7 + 6 + 4 + 5 + 5 + 8 + 2$ comm.
   $(1 + 9) + (3 + 7) + (6 + 4) + (5 + 5) + (8 + 2)$ assoc.
   $10 + 10 + 10 + 10 + 10 = 50$
6. $7 + 3 + 9 + 1 + 5 + 5 + 6 + 4 + 8$ comm.
   $(7 + 3) + (9 + 1) + (5 + 5) + (6 + 4) + 8$ assoc.
   $10 + 10 + 10 + 10 + 8 = 48$

Perplexing Properties . . . .**page 41**

1. $54 + (15 + 25)$ associative
2. 12×17 commutative
3. $66 + 85$ commutative
4. $(3 \times 24) \times 5$ associative
5. $(79 + 366) + (412 + 180)$ commutative
6. $(62 \times 8) \times 14$ associative

Multiplication Models . . . .**pages 42–43**

1. 3×6
2. 18
3. 3×5
4. 15
5. 33
6. $3 \times 6 + 3 \times 5 = 33$; yes
7. Layanna's model has the same circles, but they've been pushed together.
8. The number of columns of black and white circles combined.
9. There are 3 rows of 11 columns.
10. Yes. The circles haven't been changed.

Trading Cards . . . .**page 44**

1. 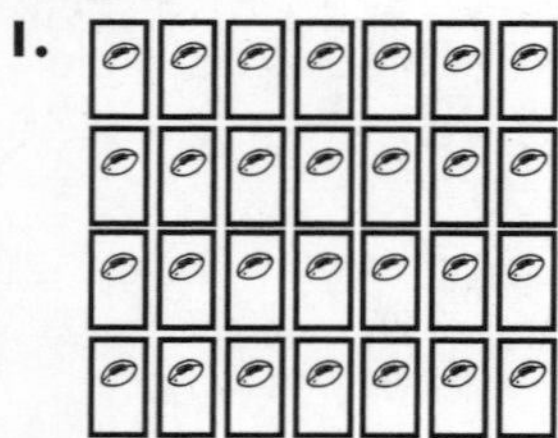
2. $4 \times 7 + 4 \times 9$
3. $28 + 36 = 64$
4.
5. 16
6. $4 \times (7 + 9)$
7. $4 \times (7 + 9) = 4 \times 16 = 64$
8. Luke changed the organization of the cards, but he still has the same number of cards. This example shows that the distributive property is true.

Daring Distributions . . . .**page 45**

1. $4 \times 12 + 4 \times 5 = 4 \times (12 + 5) = 4 \times 17$;
   Each boy will have 17 pieces of candy each.
2. $2 \times 4 + 2 \times 6 = 2 \times (4 + 6) = 2 \times 10$;
   There will be 10 stickers in each column. Keisha has 20 stickers all together.
3. $3 \times 4 + 3 \times 5 = 3 \times (4 + 5) = 3 \times 9$;
   There will be 9 cookies in each row. He baked 27 cookies all together.
4. $5 \times 15 + 5 \times 25 = 5 \times (15 + 25) = 5 \times 40$;
   There will be 40 books in each box. There are 200 books all together.

Multiplication Made Easy . . . .**pages 46–47**

1. 440
2. 162
3. 266
4. 162
5. 396
6. 402
7. 624
8. 495
9. 396
10. 715
11. 2,600
12. 913
13. 2,572
14. 927

Diligent Digits . . . .**page 48**

1. $a = 7, b = 9, c = 0, d = 8, e = 6$
2. $a = 3, b = 1, c = 6, d = 0, e = 5, f = 2, g = 4$
3. $a = 1, b = 2, c = 3, d = 4, e = 7, f = 5, g = 6, h = 8, i = 9, j = 0$
4. $a = 3, b = 7, c = 5, d = 6, e = 0, f = 2$
5. $a = 5, b = 7, c = 9, d = 3, e = 1$

Name That Digit! . . . .**page 49**

1. $a = 7, b = 8, c = 6, d = 9$
2. $e = 3, f = 1, g = 2, h = 0$
3. $a = 1, b = 5$ $c = 2, d = 4$
4. $e = 7, f = 2, g = 1$

Fruit Salad . . . .**page 50**

1. 8
2. 2
3. 9
4. 5
5. 45
6. 15
7. 3
8. 24

Answer Key

Crack the Code . . . . **page 51**
CHANGE IS THE ONLY CONSTANT

Simple Symbols . . . . **page 52**

1. = 519
2. = 416
3. = 9
4. = 1,970
5. = 837
6. = 1,135
7. = 15
8. = 576

Vintage Variables . . . . **page 53**

1. $T = 4{,}378$
2. $M = 1{,}376$
3. $K = 18$
4. $P = 1{,}423$
5. $S = 5{,}719$
6. $R = 31{,}024$
7. $N = 2{,}728$
8. $V = 9$

Doing the Two-Step . . . . **page 54**

1. $N = 7$
2. $M = 18$
3. $P = 9$
4. $Q = 48$
5. $R = 5$
6. $S = 180$

Two Is Company . . . . **page 55**

1.

b	c
5	15
15	45
8	24
36	108

2.

d	e
200	90
180	70
563	453
445	335

3.

f	g
271	257
62	466
319	209
503	25

4.

h	j
6	40
40	6
4	60
24	10

Duo Delight . . . . **page 56**

1. = 18, = 12
2. = 30, = 6
3. = 15, =32
4. = 25, = 5
5. = 360, = 615
6. = 12, = 8
7. = 8, = 13
8. = 30, = 11

Triple Triumph . . . . **page 57**

1. = 84, = 123, = 41
2. = 12, = 25, = 36
3. = 28, = 336, = 157
4. = 18, = 2, = 90

Canned Food Drive . . . . **page 58**

1. $J = 160$, $G = 90$, $C = 70$
2. $F = 400$, $T = 75$, $S = 125$
3. $R = 84$, $D = 56$, $H = 140$, $I = 280$
4. $K = 256$, $P = 216$

Something's Fishy . . . . **page 59**

1. $M = 70$, $N = 35$, $B = 95$
2. $P = 25$, $A = 30$, $T = 110$
3. $R = 20$, $C = 160$, $D = 90$
4. $G = 280$, $H = 140$, $S = 70$

Have A Ball! . . . . **page 60**

1. **a.** $D = H + 9$

b.

H	D
12	21
20	29
9	18
17	26

2. **a.** $C = D - 12$

b.

C	D
8	20
12	24
18	30
30	42

Field Trip . . . . **page 61**

1. **a.** $T = S \times 5$

b.

S	T
52	260
60	300
35	175
48	240

2. **a.** $B = P \div 28$

b.

P	B
56	2
84	3
112	4
140	5

Phone Fright . . . . **page 62**

1. Total Charged = 35 + Number of minutes used during the weekday x 0.15
2. M = number of minutes used during the weekday
3. $69.95 = 35 + M \times 0.15$
4. $M = (69.95 - 35) \div 0.15 = 233$ minutes
5. Jenna used 233 minutes during the weekdays.

Credit Catastrophe . . . . **page 63**

1. balance = unpaid amount x interest rate as a decimal + unpaid amount
2. B = balance owed
3. $B = 125 \times 0.15 + 125$
4. $B = 143.75$
5. Isaac will have a balance of $143.75.

Choice Words . . . . **pages 64–65**

1. N = number of books on the table; $788 - N = 128 \times 6$; $N = 20$; There were 20 books on the display table.
2. M = number of miles traveled; $15 + 0.25 \times M = 90$; $M = 300$; Jared's family traveled 300 miles on their trip.
3. H = number of hours worked; $6 \times H - 25 = 95$; $H = 20$; Caitlin worked 20 hours her first week.
4. T = number of tables; $7 \times T + 2 = 100$; $T = 14$; There were 14 tables set up for the banquet.

Answer Key

5. D = discount; $D = 50 \times 0.25 = 12.50$; The discount was \$12.50.
6. P = percentage discount; $250 \times P = 100$; $P = 0.40$; The bike was 40% off.
7. S = sales tax; $22 \times 0.08 = S$; $S = 1.76$; The sales tax was \$1.76.
8. B = number of full boxes of comics; $491 - 11 = 30 \times B$; $B = 16$; There are 16 full boxes of comics.

In the Fast Lane .... pages 66–67

1. 281 meters per minute; Each minute, she traveled another 281 meters.
2. 268 meters per minute; Each minute, she traveled another 268 meters.
3. $D = 281 \times T$
4. $D = 60 + 268 \times T$
5. Plug the time values into the equation to get distance values. Compare these values to the numbers in the table and make sure they match.
6. At 800 meters Miranda would win. At 1,500 meters Caroline would win.

Utterly Unknown .... pages 68–69

1. **a.** D = number of days the nail gun was rented
   b. $143 = 35 \times D + 3$; $D = (143 - 3) \div 35$; $D = 4$
   c. Danny's father rented the nail gun for 4 days.
2. **a.** $J + P = 112$
   b. $P = J + 58$
   c. $J = 27$, $P = 85$
3. **a.** $S + O = 259$
   b. $O = S + 49$
   c. $O = 154$, $S = 105$
   d. $154 = 7 \times L$ and $105 = 7 \times L$
   e. 15 lawns in September; 22 lawns in October
4. **a.** $C + S = 48$
   b. $C = 2 \times P$
   c. $C = S + 12$
   d. $C = 30$, $S = 18$, $P = 15$

Bargain Days .... pages 70–71

1. D = amount of discount; $D = 0.35 \times \$70$
2. $D = 0.35 \times 70 = 24.50$
3. Sale Price = original price – discount
4. S = sale price; $S = 70 - 24.50$
5. $S = 70 - 24.50 = 45.50$
6. Tax = tax percentage as a decimal x sale price
7. T = tax; $T = 0.06 \times 45.50$
8. $T = 0.06 \times 45.50 = 2.73$
9. Total Cost = Sale Price + Tax
10. C = Total Cost; $C = 45.50 + 2.73$
11. $C = 45.50 + 2.73 = 48.23$
12. The total cost of the skateboard, including tax, is \$48.23. Yes, the \$50 Blake has is enough to buy the skateboard.

It's A Gas, Gas, Gas! .... page 72

1. M = number of miles the car gets per gallon
2. 12 gallons x M = 360 miles
3. M = 30 miles per gallon; $M = 360 \div 12$
4. N = number of miles she can travel before running out of gas; 15 gallons x 30 miles per gallon = N miles
5. $N = 15 \times 30 = 450$ miles
6. The car can travel 30 miles on 1 gallon of gas. Cheyenne will have to stop for gas again because 15 gallons will only get her 450 miles, but she has to travel 500.

Check Your Skills .... pages 74–75

1. Samples are given below. Other answers may be correct.
   a. $17 + (92 + 12)$; associative
   b. $5 \times 50 + 5 \times 62$; distributive
   c. 16×33; commutative
2. 2,165
3. **a.**  = 1,341
   b.  = 5
   c.  = 16
   d. = 30
4. $L = 40$, $C = 35$, $H = 20$
5. **a.** $B = 12$, $D = 5$
   b. $R = 14$, $T = 7$
6. **a.** $P = 6 \times H - 25$
   b. \$215; $P = 6 \times 40 - 25 = 215$
   c. 25 hours; $125 = 6 \times H - 25$; $H = (125 + 25) \div 6 = 25$
7. **a.** C = cost of DVD; $C = 45 - 0.05 \times 45$
   b. $C = 42.75$
   c. The DVD will cost \$42.75.
8. The cost of the jacket, J, can be found using this equation. $J = 40 - 0.20 \times 40 = 40 - 8 = 32$. The cost of his purchases before tax, C, is $C = 25 + J$, or $C = 25 + 32 = 57$. The amount of the sales tax, S, can be found with this equation. $S = 0.08 \times C$ or $S = 0.08 \times 57 = 4.56$. The total price of his purchases, T, is $T = C + S$ or $T = 57 + 4.56 = \$61.56$.

Building Basics .... pages 76–77

1. $H = 3$, $L = 9$, $W = 2$
2. H = 10 ft. x 3 = 30 ft.; L = 10 ft. x 9 = 90 ft.; W = 10 ft. x 2 = 20 ft.
3.

each unit	10	12	14	16	18	20
H	30	36	42	48	54	60
L	90	108	126	144	162	180
W	20	24	28	32	36	40

Answer Key

4. $H = 3 \times U$; $L = 9 \times U$; $W = 2 \times U$
5. **a.** area
   b. 48 square units (only count the sides of the building, not the bottom or top)
   c. 144 sq. ft. (Each cube represents 12 ft. by 12 ft. of area)
   d. $S = 48 \times 144 = 6{,}912$ sq. ft.

Slippery When Wet ....pages 78–79

Answers will vary depending on experimental results.

Column Creations ....pages 80–81

1. Answers may vary.
2. Check students' columns to make sure they have the correct dimensions.
3. Experimental results may vary.
4. Check to make sure students' graphs reflect table values.
5. As the height of the column increases, the amount of weight it holds decreases.
6. Answers will vary.

How Does Your Garden Grow? ....pages 82–83

1. Answers may vary.
2. $A = 6$ square units
3. 6 units, 8 units, and 10 units
4. $N = 24$ square units
5. The area of the new garden is 4 times greater than the area of the original.
6. No. The area got 4 times bigger, not 2 times bigger.
7. The area gets 4 times bigger.
8. If the perimeter is doubled, the area will be 4 times larger.

Check Your Skills ....pages 85–86

1. $H = 4 \times U$; $h = 2 \times U$; $L = 7 \times U$; $W = 2 \times U$
2. $H = 60$ ft.; $h = 30$ ft.; $L = 105$ ft.; $W = 30$ ft.
3. $V = 148{,}500$ cu. ft.; Divide the building into 3 rectangular prisms. $V = L \times W \times h + W \times W \times h + W \times W \times h = 105 \times 30 \times 30 + 30 \times 30 \times 30 + 30 \times 30 \times 30 = 94{,}500 + 27{,}000 + 27{,}000$
4. $A = 2 \times L \times W = 2 \times 105 \times 30 = 6{,}300$ sq. ft.
5. The floor space will be 4 times larger. $4 \times 6{,}300 = 25{,}200$ sq. ft.

Go the Distance ....page 87

1. $D = R \times 90$
2. $D = 0.35 \times (\frac{90}{2}) = 15.75$ km. She can only ride out half the time she has, that way she has time to get back.
3.

R	0.25	0.275	0.3	0.325	0.35	0.375	0.4
D	22.5	24.75	27	29.25	31.5	33.75	36

4. As her speed increases, so does the distance she travels in 90 minutes.

Do You Have the Time? ....page 88

1. $D = 70 \times T$
2. $95 = 70 \times T$
   $T = \frac{95}{70}$
   $T = 1.36$ hours
3.

T	1	1.07	1.14	1.21	1.29	1.36	1.43	1.50	1.57
D	70	75	80	85	90	95	100	105	110

4. As distance increases, so does the speed.

Speed Zone page ....page 89

1. $100 = R \times T$
2. $100 = R \times 2.5$
   $R = \frac{100}{2.5}$
   $R = 40$ mph
3.

T	1.5	2	2.5	3	3.5
R	67	50	40	33	29

4. The longer the trip takes, the slower they traveled.

Coaster Chronicles ....pages 90–91

1. The height stays the same for a couple of seconds and then increases at a constant rate. This is when the rollercoaster pulls out of the staging area and gets pulled up the first big hill.
2. The ride lasts 70 seconds.
3. The riders spend more time going uphill, a total of 50 seconds of a 70 second ride.
4. At 30 seconds into the ride, the riders reach the lowest point of 10 ft.
5. At 27 seconds into the ride, the riders reach the highest point of 200 ft.
6. The Rocket is not actually shaped like the graph. The coaster has to circle back around so that riders get off at the same place they got on.
7. The roller coaster travels the fastest between 27 and 30 seconds. This shows the drop on the first big hill of the roller coaster.
8. For the first couple of seconds, the roller coaster leaves the staging area, which is 20 feet off the ground. The coaster immediately begins to climb at a steady rate to the top of a big hill, which is 200 ft. above the ground. Between 27 and 30 seconds, the coaster quickly drops down the hill to a height of 10 ft. The coaster stays level for a second or two and then begins to climb the next hill. It reaches 140 ft.—the top of the hill—at 45 seconds. Then the coaster drops to 25 ft. by 50 seconds. Between 50 and 69 seconds, the coaster rises and falls twice. The ride ends at 69 seconds, 20 ft. above the ground.

Answer Key

What's the Cost? .... **pages 92–93**

1. It would cost \$7.50 per person. \$300 ÷ 40 = \$7.50
2. $C = 300 \div P$
3.

P	C
5	60
10	30
15	20
20	15
25	12
30	10
35	8.57
40	7.50

P	C
45	6.67
50	6
55	5.45
60	5
65	4.62
70	4.29
75	4

4. The cost per person decreases as the number of people increases.
5. Answers may vary.
6.

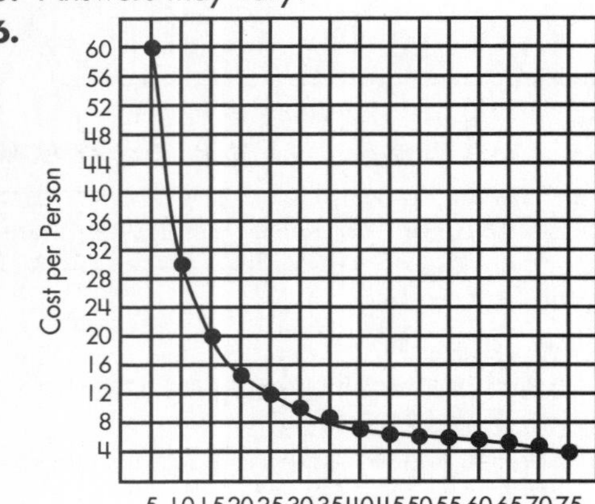

Discount Extravaganza .... **pages 94–95**

1. \$11.25; 0.25 x 45 = 11.25
2. $D = 0.25 \times P$
3.

P	5	10	15	20	25	30	35	40	45	50
D	1.25	2.50	3.75	5	6.25	7.5	8.75	10	11.25	12.50

4.

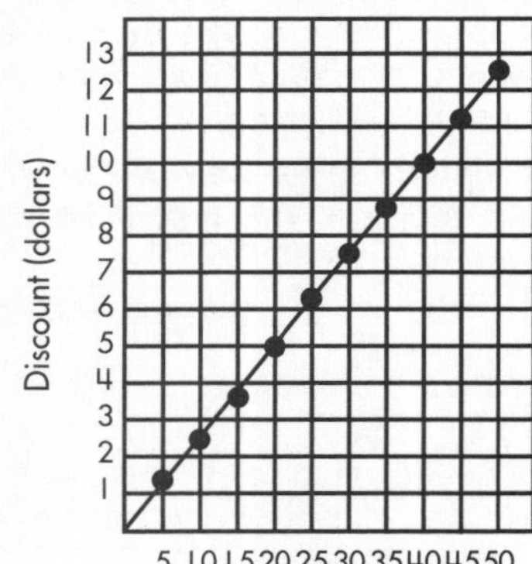

5. When the original price increases by \$5, the discount increases by \$1.25.
6. \$33.75; \$45 – 0.25 x 45 = 45 – 11.25 = 33.75
7. $S = P - 0.25 \times P$
8.

P	5	10	15	20	25	30	35	40	45	50
S	3.75	7.50	11.25	15	18.75	22.50	26.25	30	33.75	37.50

9.

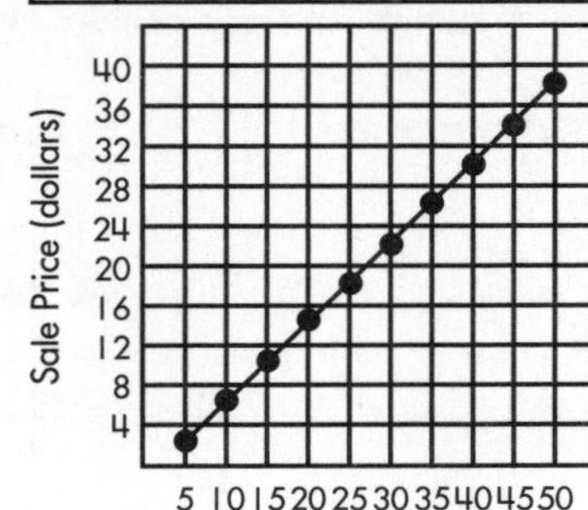

10. As the original price increases by \$5, the sale price increases by \$3.75.

A Bit of Bounce .... **pages 96–97**

1.

# bounces	0	1	2	3	4	5	6
height (ft.)	16	12	9	6.8	5.1	3.8	2.8

2.

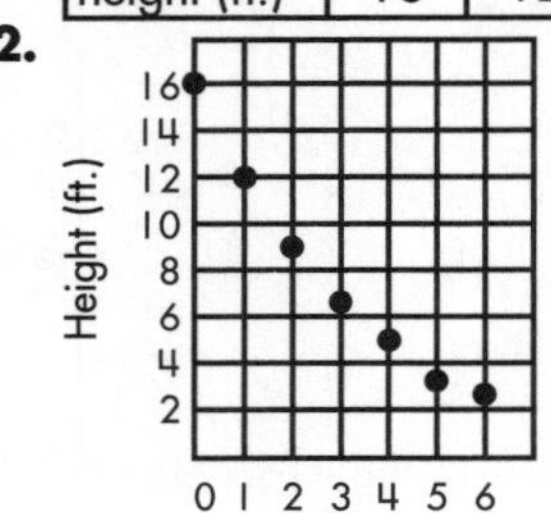

3. change: – 4, – 3, – 2.2, – 1.7, – 1.3, – 1; decreasing rate of change
4. There is a smaller vertical space between each pair of points from left to right.
5.

# bounces	0	1	2	3	4	5	6
height (ft.)	16	8	4	2	1	0.5	0.25

6.

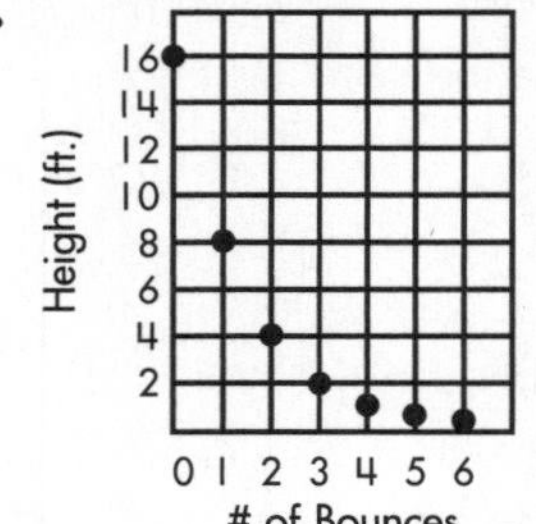

The height decreases at a decreasing rate. The difference in height from one value to the next gets smaller each time.

Answer Key

Aquarium Arrangements ....pages 98–99

1. $V = 19 \times 74 \times H = 1{,}406 \times H$
2.

H (in.)	24	25	26	27	28	29	30
V (in.3)	33,744	35,150	36,556	37,962	39,368	40,774	42,180

3. When the height increases by 1 inch, the volume increases by 1,406 cubic inches.
4. The volume changes at a constant rate. The difference between every pair of numbers for volume is 1,406.
5.

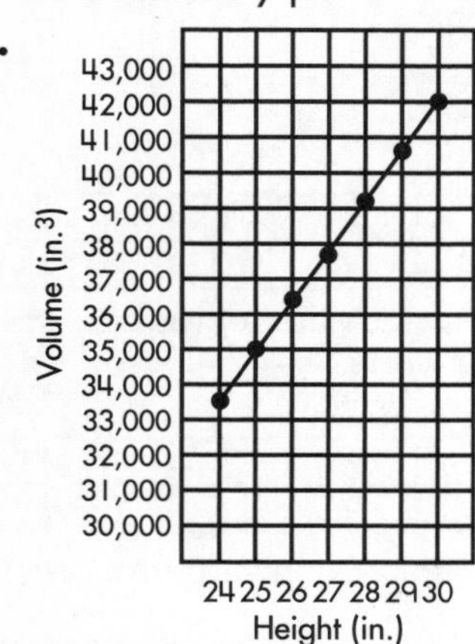

6. The graph is a straight line. The vertical distance between each set of points is always the same. This shows that the volume increases at a constant rate.

Payment Plans ....pages 100–101

1. Answers may vary.
2. $M = 3 \times D$
3.

# of days	1	2	3	4	5	6	7	8	9	10	11	12	13	14	15
total earned	3	6	9	12	15	18	21	24	27	30	33	36	39	42	45

4. Constant rate. The total earned increases by $3/day.
5.

# days	1	2	3	4	5	6	7	8	9	10	11	12
amt.	.01	.02	.04	.08	.16	.32	.64	1.28	2.56	5.12	10.24	20.48
total	.01	.03	.07	.15	.31	.63	1.27	2.55	5.11	10.23	20.47	40.95

6. Varying rate. The total increases by a different amount each time.
7. The first plan would be better. Miguel would make $20 compared to $10.23.
8. The second plan would be better. Miguel would make $327.67, which is a lot more than $30.
9. Miguel should accept his mother's plan if he works less than 12 days.
10. Miguel would do better with his own plan if he works 12 days or more.

What Goes Up Must Come Down .....pages 102–103

1. about 6 ft.
2. about 0.9 seconds, at 33 ft.
3. about 1.9 seconds
4.

T	0.1	0.3	0.5	0.7	0.9	1.1	1.3	1.5	1.7	1.9
H	10	19	27	31	33	31	27	19	10	0

5. 0 sec. to 0.9 sec
6. decreasing rate; The difference between the heights gets smaller each time as it approaches the maximum height.
7. 0.9 sec. to 2.0 sec.
8. increasing rate; The difference between the heights gets larger each time as the height of the ball decreases.

Phone Tree ....pages 104–105

1.

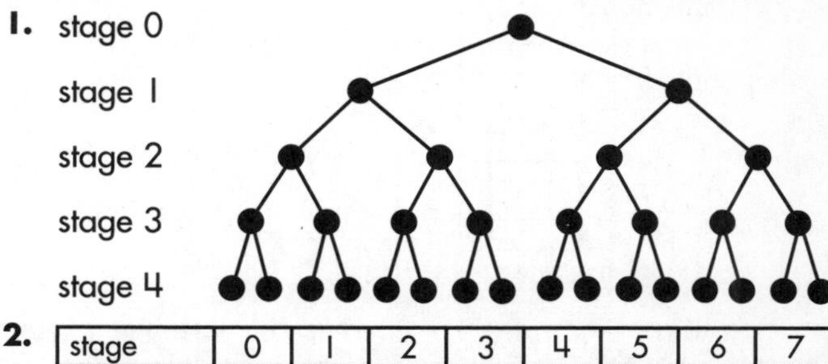

2.

stage	0	1	2	3	4	5	6	7
# calls	1	2	4	8	16	32	64	128

3.

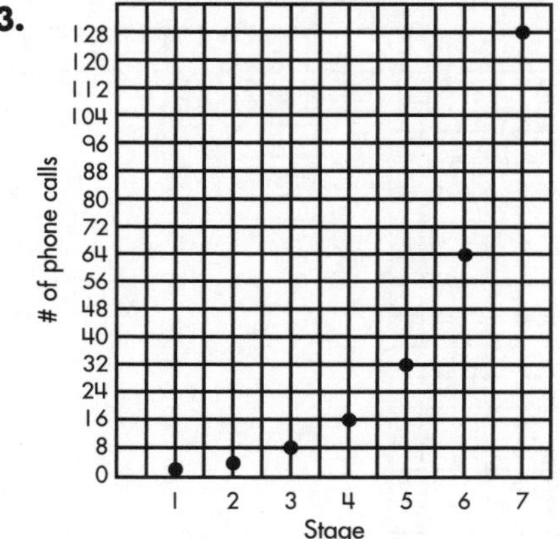

4. The number of calls increases at an increasing rate. The difference between the number of calls from one stage to the next gets larger and larger.
5. From left to right, the vertical space between each pair of points gets larger (it doubles). This means the rate of change is increasing.

Check Your Skills ....pages 107–108

1. **a.** $D = 65 \times T$

   b.

time	1	2	3	4	5	6	7	8
distance	65	130	195	260	325	390	455	520

   c. The distance increases by 65 miles when the time increases by 1 hour.

   d. constant rate; distance increase 65 miles each hr.

Answer Key

2. a.

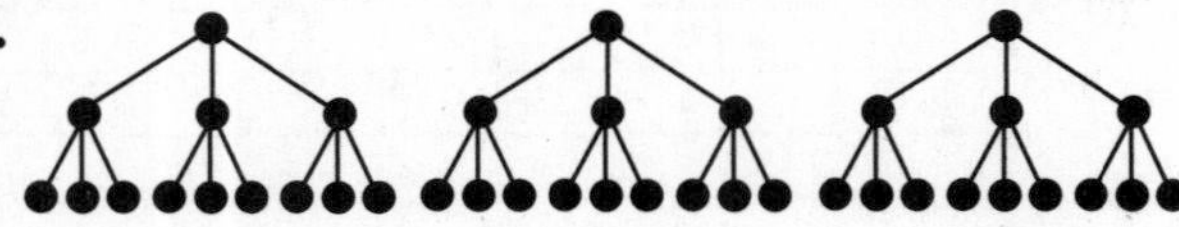

b.

stage	0	1	2	3	4	5
# calls	1	3	9	27	81	243

c.

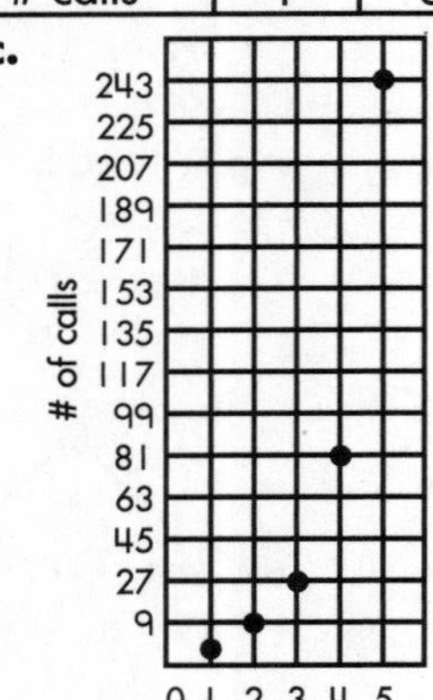

d. increasing rate; The difference between the number of calls from one stage to the next gets larger each time.

3. a.

# bounces	0	1	2	3	4	5	6	7	8
height (in.)	72	48	32	21.3	14.2	9.5	6.3	4.2	2.8

b.

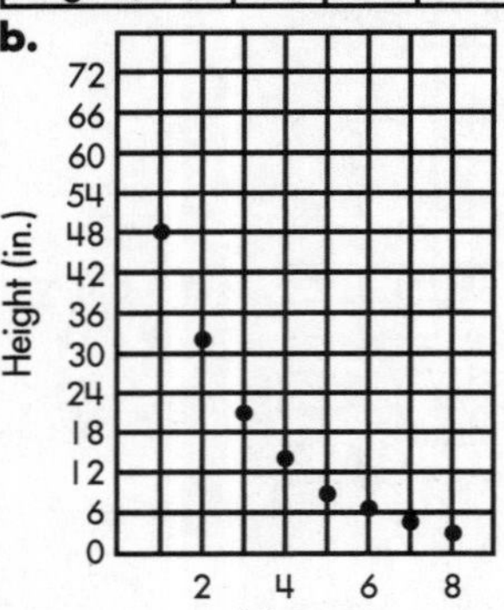

c. decreasing rate; The difference between the heights from one bounce to the next gets smaller each time.

4. a. increasing rate

b. constant rate

c. decreasing rate

1. a. 26, 33, 41; Start with 1 and add the next consecutive integer each time.

b. 196, 317, 513; The next number will be the sum of the previous 2 numbers.

c. 24, 27, 30; Add 3 each time. This pattern has a constant rate.

2.

IN	10	6	15	22	18	44
OUT	22	18	27	34	30	56

Rule: OUT = IN + 12

3. a. = 48, = 6

b. = 60, = 5

4. a. $O = 100 - 5 \times W$

b. O = $55

c. W = 12 weeks

d. As the number of weeks increases by 1, the amount Alita owes decreases by $5.

5. a.

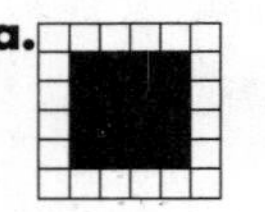 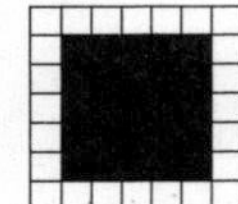

b.

stage	0	1	2	3	4	5
white	8	12	16	20	24	28

c. The number of white squares increases at a constant rate of 4 squares per stage.

d.

stage	0	1	2	3	4	5
black	1	4	9	16	25	36

e. The number of black squares increases at an increasing rate.

f. white squares: Graph II; black squares: Graph III

repeating pattern	**growing pattern**
decreasing pattern	**rule**
constant rate	**varying rate**

a series of numbers that gets larger using a rule

5, 9, 13, 17, 21 Rule: + 4

a series of numbers, letters, shapes, or other objects that repeat in a certain order

3 3 4 4

A A B B

describes the process used to create a pattern or function

– 10
or OUT = IN x 3

a series of numbers that gets smaller using a rule

35, 33, 32, 30, 28 Rule: – 2

when a variable changes by different amounts each time

time	distance
1	10
2	14
3	19
4	26
5	35

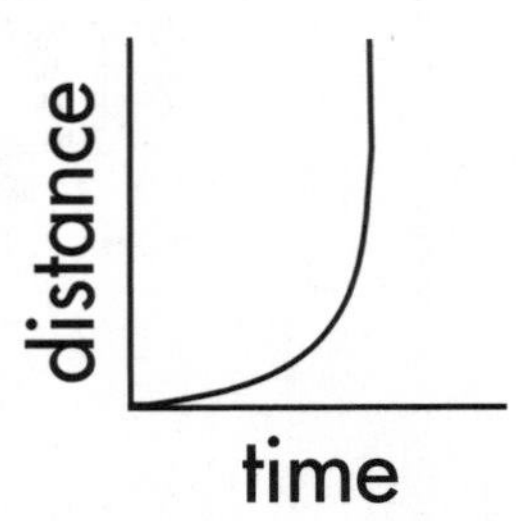

when a variable changes by the same amount each time

time	distance
1	10
2	20
3	30
4	40

distance
time

function machine

commutative property

associative property

distributive property

order of operations

variable

changing the order of the numbers does not change the answer

7 x 4 = 4 x 7
28 = 28

5 + 9 = 9 + 5
14 = 14

uses a rule to change IN numbers to OUT numbers

IN	55	38	72	61	80
OUT	26	9	43	32	51

Rule: OUT = IN – 29

a way to rewrite multiplication over addition without changing the answer

3 x (5 + 7) = 3 x 5 + 3 x 7
3 x 12 = 15 + 21
36 = 36

changing the grouping of the numbers does not change the answer

(14 + 12) + 8 = 14 + (12 + 8)
26 + 8 = 14 + 20
34 = 34

a letter or symbol that stands for an unknown number

3 x (T) = 18

tells in which sequence operations should be performed to get the right answer

Parentheses, Exponents, Multiplication, Division, Addition, Subtraction

distance equation

model

area of a rectangle

equivalent

rate

coordinate graph

using objects, sketches, or mathematical equations to represent a situation

shows the relationship between distance traveled, average speed, and time

$D = R \times T$

has the same value, but is written differently

$5 + T = 10$ means the same as $T = 10 - 5$

A = L x W

a graph using points to show the relationship between two variables

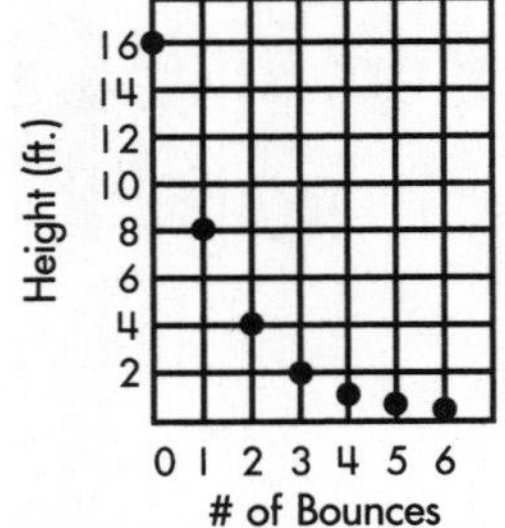

a comparison of two different kinds of units

miles per hour
dollars per hour
hours per week

increasing rate of change

decreasing rate of change

volume of a rectangular prism

sum

product

difference

the difference between each pair of numbers gets smaller

Time (sec)	0.1	0.3	0.5	0.7	0.9
Height (ft)	10	20	27	31	33

How does the height change?

the difference between each pair of numbers gets larger

Time (sec)	1.1	1.3	1.5	1.7	1.9
Height (ft)	31	27	20	10	3

How does the height change?

the answer to an addition problem

82 + 35 = (117)

V = L x W x H

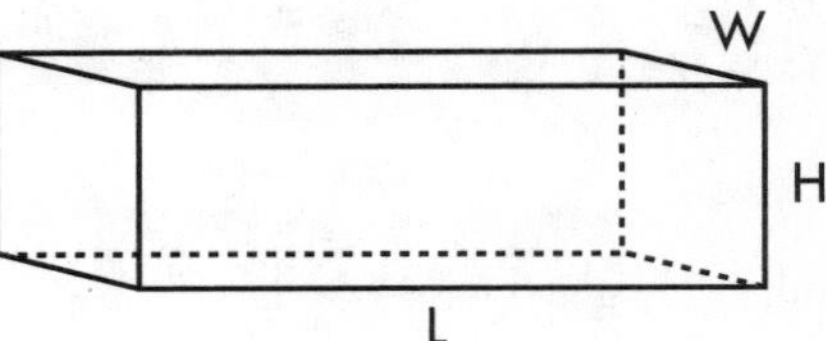

the answer to a subtraction problem

117 − 82 = (35)

the answer to a multiplication problem

3 x 14 = (42)